YOUR MESS,
GOD'S
MASTERPIECE

FIND THE TRIUMPHANT LIFE
YOUR HEART IS SEARCHING FOR

YOUR MESS, GOD'S MASTERPIECE

Derek Webster

PARACLETE PRESS
Brewster, Massachusetts

2021 First Printing

Your Mess, God's Masterpiece: Find the Triumphant Life Your Heart is Searching For

Copyright © 2021 by Derek Webster

ISBN 978-64060-1-549-7

Figures that appear in the book are the design of the author.

The Paraclete Press name and logo (dove on cross) are trademarks of Paraclete Press.

   Library of Congress Cataloging-in-Publication Data
Names: Webster, Derek H., author.
Title: Your mess, God's masterpiece : find the triumphant life your heart
  is searching for / Derek Webster.
Description: Brewster, Massachusetts : Paraclete Press, [2021] | Includes
  bibliographical references. | Summary: "Viewed through the lens of the
  story of Joseph, this book offers advice and examples how God can use
  dysfunction to give us opportunities for health, and calm to our
  chaos"-- Provided by publisher.
Identifiers: LCCN 2020032420 (print) | LCCN 2020032421 (ebook) | ISBN
  9781640605497 (trade paperback) | ISBN 9781640605503 (epub) | ISBN
  9781640605510 (pdf)
Subjects: LCSH: Joseph (Son of Jacob) | Self-actualization
  (Psychology)--Religious aspects--Christianity. | Consolation. |
  Health--Religious aspects--Christianity.
Classification: LCC BS580.J6 W36 2021 (print) | LCC BS580.J6 (ebook) |
  DDC 248.4--dc23
LC record available at https://lccn.loc.gov/2020032420
LC ebook record available at https://lccn.loc.gov/2020032421

10 9 8 7 6 5 4 3 2 1

Published by Paraclete Press
Brewster, Massachusetts
www.paracletepress.com
Printed in the United States of America

This book is dedicated to anyone who has ever stopped, looked around, and wondered how they got here and where they're going.

CONTENTS

INTRODUCTION
Going from Mess to Masterpiece ix

PART ONE
YOUR MESS

1 **Trapped by My Life** 3

2 **It's Their Fault** 15

3 **Maybe Some of This Is Me** 29

4 **The Mess Good Choices Can Bring** 43

5 **Letting Go** 61

6 **Where was God?** 75

PART TWO
HIS MASTERPIECE

7 **My Life is Turning Around!** 87

8 **Renegotiating Relationships** 105

9 **Forgiving and Wisdom** 121

10 **Forging a New Life Together** 137

11 **A New View!** 149

12 **More Ahead** 175

ACKNOWLEDGMENTS 183

ABOUT THE AUTHOR 184

LINKS AND NOTES 185

Going from Mess to Masterpiece

I know something about you. You feel like Humpty Dumpty. You're worried that "all the king's horses and all the king's men" won't be able to make whole the pieces of your life scattered around you. You can't talk about it, because you don't want to concern the people around you. But you wonder if your destiny is obscurity, brokenness, and frustration. You're not alone.

So many find themselves stuck in a world full of dysfunctional associations and circumstances. I recently binged a Netflix documentary series about cheerleaders. The series (*Cheer*, 2020) follows a community college that has won multiple cheerleading national titles. These are incredible athletes. But episode after episode reflected the true-life stories of cheerleaders emerging from dysfunctional families. One young woman was left with her brother to survive alone in a trailer when she was in high school. Her father married another woman who had children and determined there was no space in his life to include his own in his new, mixed family. He left his son and daughter to fend for themselves. Taken in by her grandparents, she struggled with feelings of isolation and abandonment. Another young man lived in a house where he was often made fun of by his many half-brothers and sisters. The stories were heart-wrenching.

This book is designed to help you move out of that world to a world of healthy relationships and perspectives. It may not change your circumstances immediately, but it can give you the confidence and tools to begin moving from them to a better life.

After nearly thirty years of working with others in pastoral roles, I can help you move toward wholeness. Actually, that's a partial truth. The Bible can help you move toward wholeness. My job is to help you slow down and pay attention to what is there.

A friend of mine once commented, "Every sermon is the same. We're all saying, 'Love God, hate sin.'" And in one sense he's right. You know that to move from brokenness to wholeness, things have to change. You've probably advised yourself countless times about the difference between what is happening and what should be happening. The reason you're not moving forward isn't that you're uncertain something needs to change, but that you're unsure how to get there. At the same time, you know that things can't continue as they are. You're stuck. You need some outside help to coach you through to the life you're longing for. This book is here to help you get there.

I once ate spaghetti and didn't know I had a miniature Jackson Pollock painting of spaghetti sauce all over my tie. When I preached that evening, no one mentioned anything to me about it until the end of the night. They allowed me to publicly embarrass and distract others by the mess I'd inadvertently made simply by choosing to remain silent. I want something better for you. I want to help by pointing out the metaphorical spaghetti on your tie and offering you a way to fix it. In the case of spaghetti, the solution is to change neckties. I wish all of the messes we experience had as simple a solution.

Scientists once built a gun to launch four-pound dead chickens at the windshields of commercial airplanes, military jets, and the space shuttle. Chickens shot through the air, all traveling at the highest velocity possible. The idea was to simulate what happens when birds hit an aircraft to ensure the windshields could withstand the force of the impact. It was quite an original idea.

Across the Atlantic, British engineers heard about the gun. They wanted to test it on the windshields of their new high-speed trains. The Americans sent a gun to the British engineers. After they fired the gun, the British engineers stood dumbfounded. The chicken shot out of the barrel and smashed the "shatter-proof" windshield to pieces, careened through the control console, snapped the engineer's backrest in two, and embedded itself in the back wall of the cabin. The British then sent NASA the disastrous results of the experiment along with the designs of the windshield and asked the U.S. scientists if they had any suggestions. Their response was a one-line memo: "Defrost the chicken."

What's the point? Dysfunction is like a chicken hurtling through the air at us. How can we defrost the chicken so that when it impacts our lives, it doesn't create an unmanageable mess and wreck the train? We all have to live with dysfunction. But the impact of dysfunction upon our lives can be less damaging.

But let me warn you. You'll be frustrated at times as you read what's ahead. You'll say to yourself, *I know this already! Let's just move on to what I should do.* You won't want to stop and reflect. You'll start looking for a sentence, a short-cut, or a simplification to move forward. But like a good therapist, pastor, or coach, I'm here to show that which you don't want to see. You'll have to face some things you don't want to face. There will be times we'll have to change our focus from Joseph to others, and you'll ask why we're wasting our time with them. But there's a reason for every page in this book. If you stay with it, I promise you by the end, you'll see why I directed your attention to the people and the details you might not otherwise consider.

This book is designed to parallel the journey from dysfunction to health using the biblical story of Joseph. Why Joseph? The story of Joseph is a story not only of moving from slavery to power, but also of how messes can become masterpieces. Joseph changed from a world of broken relationships to one of healthy relationships. He was transformed from the inside out, and against all the odds. That's the kind of victory we all aspire to achieve. We think of Joseph as an extraordinary person. But the Bible sees Joseph as an ordinary person that God made exceptional.

Most of the world has seen plays or heard musicals about Joseph's story. For example, there was a time when Donnie Osmond, with perfect teeth, was virtually synonymous with Andrew Lloyd

Weber's blockbuster production *Joseph and the Amazing Technicolor Dreamcoat*. Joseph's story also appears in at least three major world religions: Judaism, Christianity, and Islam. Most people are familiar with Joseph's story in one way or another. Here's what most know about his story:

- It involved a coat of many colors.
- Joseph was betrayed and enslaved.
- Joseph became a powerful man in Egypt.

Are we helpless in the face of dysfunction, or can we do something about it? And what about God? Is God indifferent to our messes, or does he care about them? The story of Joseph reminds us of what we can and can't control, how and why God uses circumstances and people to grow us, and how we can be proactive along the way.

The challenge of familiarity with any story is that it can breed impatience. We race ahead to what we think we know instead of actually working our way through the text. But the text is where the insights are. Scripture reminds us that God longs to step into our mess. There's nothing too messy for God to redeem. And though it's a story rooted in a religious text, you don't have to be particularly religious to appreciate it. The good news is that it's a great story. The great news is that it's also the story of someone on a personal journey from frustration to victory. That person is you.

The Journey We're Taking Together

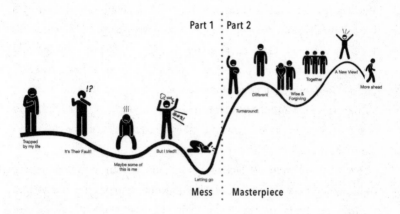

The first part of this book is an in-depth look at the messes that surround us and the messes we're in. The temptation is to say, *I get it: life is messy. Let's move on.* But each stage and aspect requires examination because it's in the context of the mess that we find the victory. There's a reason that a counselor will ask you to go back and recount your past. The purpose isn't to listen to a yarn. The aim is to look closer so that you can see insights from your history that have held you captive and re-cast them so that they no longer hold sway in your present. The apostle Paul puts this in terms of "taking off" specific patterns of beliefs, behaviors, or characteristics. If you already knew how to do this, you'd have done it already. The purpose of Part One is to wade into the mess so that you can move forward.

Managing a blessing can be as challenging as managing a curse. Part Two is where Joseph's life turns around dramatically. But remember, the story of Joseph isn't a story about finding one victory. There was not a single battle that Joseph fought and won. His story is one of how potential is realized. As Joseph was changed in the process, he had to renegotiate aspects of his life. It's incredibly challenging when the past tries to dictate our future. For better and worse, we're all creatures of habit. But whereas in part one God moved Joseph from the mess, in part two Joseph rewired his world based on what he had learned through his messes. We'll look at how he did it, and how you can too.

Structurally, each chapter has standard components. The figure above gives you a good idea of each step, moving from feeling defeated and trapped by life to a new vista in victorious living. You'll notice that we end in a "higher" place than where we began. Think of the line as a road leading into high mountains. The journey you're taking is leading you from the valley to the mountaintop. I'll point out the issue or theme we want to examine in the light of the progression of the journey.

Then we'll explore the biblical text and discover how that theme applies to Joseph's story. Finally, I'll point out where you're likely right and wrong about that theme and the application of it in your life. I'll give you some lessons to remember and apply.

At the end of each chapter, there are application questions for you to work through. Think of these questions as your personal homework between sessions. If you need to read through the whole book before going back and revisiting each chapter's applications, that's fine. But the book is designed to help you work through each chapter in succession. Like any story, where you are now depends on where you were, and where you're going depends on where you are. So much of life is trying to put together a mosaic from the broken pieces our lives become.

There are no shortcuts to change. Each of you is on a journey of divine design. But if you'll pay attention and follow God closely, there's a pathway to a better life.

PART ONE
YOUR MESS

1

Trapped by My Life

"Status quo, you know, is Latin for 'the mess we're in.'" —Ronald Reagan

■

"Jacob lived in the land of his father's sojournings, in the land of Canaan. . . . [Joseph] was a boy with the sons of Bilhah and Zilpah, his father's wives." —Genesis 37:1–2

Trapped
by my life

Years ago when I was in Austria, I spoke with a young man whose marriage was failing. He told me their union was suffering because of the severe trauma he had faced when he was young. I gently inquired what type of damage he was working through. "Birth," he replied earnestly. His mother had told him his birth itself was so traumatic that he required ongoing therapy to overcome it. As his marriage was falling apart, he had a convenient scapegoat. "I'm not a jerk. I was traumatized by my birth." I don't want to give the impression that I'm mocking this young man. I'm not. But our circumstances are not the scapegoats we make them out to be.

In one sense, we're all a product of our circumstances. And there's little we can do to control the circumstances into which we were born. Some are born in shantytowns, others in mansions. We can't pretend that circumstances don't matter.

My father used to have a phrase in his sermons that grew famous in our family lore. He would say, "Back in the Ozarks of Missoura" (never MissourEE, but MissourAH). And then he would pull out a farming or ranching principle and apply it to the message. I knew from stories of his past that he had learned to ride and break horses and milk cows on their farm in the Ozarks. I knew he, his three brothers, and one sister had grown up poor but happy. To hear him talk about it, one might think he was a country boy who moved to the big city. But he had only spent five years of his childhood in Missouri. Dad was a Californian.

Many years later, I surprised dad with a father-son trip to the Ozarks. He was excited, and as we drove there, he regaled me with stories from his time there. After visiting the old family farm and giving him some time to wistfully see the old barn, I commented, "You must have really loved it here." His reply floored me. "Not really," he said. I asked, "Well, why do you refer to your time here so often." He shrugged and said, "They were my formative years."

Everyone has a context from which they emerge. Many people feel completely trapped by their circumstances because they spend so much time reacting to them. We all deal with what's thrown at us and we adjust.

When COVID-19 hit Illinois, the governor called for a statewide house quarantine. The circumstances dictated our response, which was a restriction on our freedom to move freely around. When unemployment increased, what was blamed? The circumstances.

In the ancient world, our ancestors blamed the stars or the gods. Today, some blame their horoscopes. Born under a sign, the ancients believed that the heavens gave them no choice but the lives they were living. Some physicists and philosophers today, under the auspices of evolutionary theory, think that mathematics or some numerical lottery has pre-determined all the choices you will ever make. If we're to move forward, we have to find a way to understand and address our circumstances. No therapist ever told a client that their personal historical context has no bearing on their condition.

Joseph's Circumstances

Imagine being a part of the most significant family in history. There are some well-known families, such as the Rockefellers, Clintons, Bushes, or Kennedys. But they are nothing compared to the legacy of Joseph's family. To understand Joseph, you have to first know about Abraham,

Isaac, and Jacob. It's impossible to study Joseph without understanding his context. Joseph was born into an immigrant family with a prominent and important history.

Abraham, Sarah, and God's Promise

Joseph's great-grandfather was Abraham. Scripture tells of the amazing faith Abraham had and describes him as "the father of us all" (Rom. 4:16; Gal. 3:7–9). "By faith Abraham obeyed when he was called to go out to a place that he was to receive as an inheritance. And he went out, not knowing where he was going. By faith he went to live in the land of promise, as in a foreign land, living in tents with Isaac and Jacob, heirs with him of the same promise. For he was looking forward to the city that has foundations, whose designer and builder is God" (Heb. 11:8–10).

In Genesis 12, God told Abraham he wanted to bless the nations (the world) through him. So, Abraham left his hometown of Ur and traveled to where God wanted him to go. God was leading Abraham to establish a new nation.

God made a specific promise to Abraham. In Genesis 15, God promised that he would give Abraham a family and that his family would be huge. His descendants would become too many to count. They would be as numerous as stars in the universe or the grains of sand in a desert. God also promised Abraham land, which was a big deal in the ancient world. God would gift to Abraham territory where his descendants could flourish. But God's most significant promise was that through Abraham's seed, Jesus, the world would find salvation by faith (Gal. 3:8–9, 16–18).

Abraham trusted God to deliver on his promise. The problem was that his wife, Sarah, couldn't have children and was growing old. It's hard to have a lot of descendants if you can't produce even one! Sarah came up with the wrong solution. She suggested that Abraham sleep with her servant, a woman named Hagar.

Hagar gave birth to a son named Ishmael. Unfortunately, Sarah's solution created greater relational chaos. Perhaps you've heard of the phrases "God helps those who help themselves" or "the ends justify the means." But neither of those are true. God cares about trusting him for the results he promises. When we rush ahead, this can create more significant problems than those with which we began.

When Sarah became pregnant at an advanced age with Isaac, Abraham cast out his old family for his new family. Hagar and Ishmael were sent away. His love was with Sarah. Moreover, the promise and blessing of God would go through Sarah. Abraham and Sarah's dysfunctional family choices created a whole range of unhealthy consequences. To this day, the enmity between Israel and her neighbors is a product of that decision. Abraham and Sarah had one child, Isaac.

Isaac and Rebekah

Isaac was Joseph's grandfather. Isaac married Rebekah, and God reiterated his promise to Isaac. God was going to bless them. Isaac and Rebecca had twin sons: Esau and Jacob.

Isaac and Rebekah each had their favorites. Playing favorites with your children is a recipe for disaster. Isaac loved Esau. Esau was a man's man. In modern terms, he was the captain. He was a hairy hunter and the eldest of the twins. Because Esau was older, it was his right to receive the inheritance of his father and the blessing of God. Esau was also ruled by his emotions and focused on the present.

Rebekah had other plans. Jacob was a momma's boy who learned how to cook. Jacob preferred the indoors to the outdoors and herding to hunting. He was smart and cunning, thoughtful, and focused on the future. Jacob used those differences to leverage Esau's inheritance away. Esau traded his inheritance for stew. Jacob must have been a great cook.

Meanwhile, Rebekah worked against her husband, Isaac, to make sure that her favorite son, Jacob, received Isaac's blessing. Together they tricked Isaac. Jacob wound up with both the inheritance and the promise as a result. Esau and Jacob would have a strained relationship from then on.

Isaac and Rebekah weren't always on the same page, either. But they agreed on at least one thing: Jacob needed to find a wife. So, they sent Jacob away to Jacob's uncle, Laban. There, on Laban's ranch, Jacob fell in love with Rachel, Laban's youngest daughter. He would love her for the rest of his life. But Jacob, who tricked Esau, got tricked by Laban.

Jacob, Leah, and Rachel, and Their Handmaidens

Jacob's first wife was Rachel's sister, Leah. The Bible says that Leah had weak eyes. That's a polite way of saying she wasn't attractive. Laban couldn't marry her off, so he tricked Jacob into marrying her first. On the day of Jacob's wedding, Laban substituted Rachel with Leah. In that ancient culture, the women wore a veil the groom wouldn't be able to see through. After the wedding and the party that followed, Jacob didn't discover who he'd married until the next morning. Jacob worked seven years to marry Rachel but woke up with Leah. Laban wasn't exactly a good uncle.

But Jacob loved Rachel. He loved her with all his heart. Rachel is the one for whom he'd yearned and labored for years. His heart had always belonged to her. Jacob was so in love with Leah's sister that he worked another seven years to marry her. Sadly, from the moment they married, Leah was desperate for Jacob's love. But Jacob couldn't give Leah a love he didn't have for her. His heart belonged to her younger sister.

The ancient world was in some ways like the modern world. Sometimes when people find themselves in broken marriages, they think that having kids will solve their marital issues. The hope is that the kids will draw the parents' dysfunction together toward health. It doesn't work that way, but still, a lot of people keep trying that approach. Leah started to have kids, and her whole idea was, *If I have kids, then Jacob will love me. If I give him sons, then he'll look at me and think, "Well, hey, you're not so bad. Though it's not ideal, I'm going to choose to love you too."* Life is full of hopes like that. Most of them aren't realistic. Jacob just couldn't bring himself to love Leah. His heart belonged to Rachel.

You might be thinking, *the Bible is okay with polygamy*. Take a look at this family. The Bible is not okay with it. In the movie *White Christmas* (1954) there's a duet by two sisters who sing, "Lord help the mister who comes between me and my sister. And Lord help the sister who comes between me and my man." Jacob was the man between these two sisters.

The marital situation was an unfortunate marriage dynamic that would turn into an unhealthy family dynamic. Perhaps that's one reason the Bible tells us marriage is best between one husband and one wife.

Leah and Rachel had handmaidens who were helpers for them, and Jacob had relations with all of them. The result was a slew of boys with four different women committed to two different teams, with each side spearheaded by two sister wives, Leah and Rachel. Leah's helper was Zilpah, and Rachel's helper was Bilhah. All four of these women—Leah, Zilpah, Bilhah, and Rachel—gave Jacob sons. Joseph was one of them.

Joseph was born into a particular context. There were patterns of generational sins. Despite being in the most significant family in history, Joseph suffered from the effects of the good and bad choices of others. Family played an essential role in this particular mess.

Maybe your mess includes family mess too. Perhaps you were born into the kind of mess that makes you a little ashamed to be around happy families. Maybe the best two-word description is "it's complicated."

My wife will tell you that her family is complicated. Her maiden name was Lopez, but she was not of Mexican descent. Her grandmother was pregnant by a man whom she did not want to marry. She would never divulge any details about the baby's biological father. Then her grandmother married her grandfather, who was of Mexican descent; his last name was Lopez. Melissa comes from a complicated family full of stepbrothers, stepfathers, and half-cousins.

But keep this in mind: Complicated isn't the same thing as ugly. It just means that things aren't as straightforward as they may appear. If you're embarrassed about your family, remember that God chose complicated families through which to work out his plan of redemption.

Or maybe your family is less complicated. Perhaps you were raised in a Christian home where everyone on the outside thought your family was perfect. You might have one mom, one dad, and an extended family where no one has divorced, and no one appears to have any major vices. Others may look at your Instagram family photos and think your family is perfect. If they only knew.

I grew up in a less-complicated family. Both of my parents were Christ-followers. I have a younger sister, whom I love. As I was growing up, Julie Andrews (who starred in the 1964 movie *Mary Poppins*) was an admired actress. She played the perfect fictional character of a nanny and a friend. She sang her way through difficulties and made things fun for others. My mom was like Julie Andrews in *The Sound of Music*, only better. We grew up singing as a family quartet in churches. Mom could make anyone laugh and think and love deeper. She loved Jesus. My dad was a soldier, businessman, and pastor. Dad was a thinker and raised us to think for ourselves. He often encouraged my sister and me with the words that we could be anything to which we set our minds and hearts. Dad always reminded us to put Jesus first in everything. In some ways, we were an uncomplicated family. But that didn't mean we were consistently a healthy family.

Joseph's family lived in the land of Canaan, surrounded by pagans. My wife and our family have lived overseas. When you move and live as immigrants, the positive is that you share a collective experience. The family pulls together. Joseph was born into a tight-knit, prominent family, but that didn't make it an idyllic family. Joseph was born into a fragmented dynamic. The negative of living as immigrants is there is little recourse to go outside of the immediate family for support. Joseph seemed literally trapped. Born into a complicated family in a place surrounded by those who didn't think his family belonged there, Joseph was alienated twice over.

Circumstances and You

Whenever you blame your life on your circumstances, you're only partially right. Yes, life is unfair. Your circumstances determine the people, places, or positions you'll have to overcome. Helen Keller once said, "Character cannot be developed in ease and quiet. Only through experience of trial and suffering can the soul be strengthened, ambition inspired, and success achieved." Circumstances dealt Helen Keller a bitter blow. At two years old, due to an unforeseen illness, she was left deaf and blind. Yet, she did not allow circumstances to feed her resentment.

I meet people from a variety of difficult backgrounds. Some came from events so challenging one might think they could never emerge from them whole. And yet, after all of these years of ministry, I can say definitively that the circumstances aren't the best indication of character. There are people born with tremendous advantages who choose to be trapped by life. So, while blaming your life on circumstances is partially true, it's not necessarily the determiner of your responses. Some of the kindest people I've met have emerged from the most horrific of childhoods. Others had idyllic childhoods. The circumstances of your birth or life need not be the scapegoat for your responses. But how to get from resentment to gratitude?

A Chinese proverb says, "A journey of a thousand miles begins with one step." Let's take one step together by applying our first lessons.

Lessons from Joseph's Family Context and History

1. See the context in which you were born.

It takes courage to see things as they are and not as we hope them to be. Sometimes, our memory is selective. I've been told, "I had an idyllic childhood. Everything was great all the time. My adult life is kind of screwed up, but my childhood was amazing." Indeed, our past doesn't necessarily determine our future. We can be raised in happy homes and still make bad choices! But we also tend to gloss over family dysfunction. We don't pause to think about generational patterns and how we reap the seeds others have sown. None of us are born in a perfect vacuum.

We allow our memories to rewrite history rather than learn from it. The truth is, dysfunction exists even in the best families. Sin still does damage.

I was a highly intentional father. Surely, if any children would have zero baggage, it would be my children. They were raised in a home with me as their dad! When my sons were young, I thought I'd worked out the perfect recipe for fatherhood. I thought I was doing everything right.

But with time, I've learned to recognize that there's plenty of baggage to go around. My kids carry around baggage. It doesn't mean they weren't loved or raised in a God-centric environment. It just means that none of us can predict what luggage others will carry as we move through the journey. Things tend to get packed in and lugged around that we cannot predict or avoid. All we can do is to recognize and deal with that baggage appropriately and as it reveals itself.

Don't excuse the bad parts of your circumstances. Don't pretend that the bad is somehow relabeled as good. I'm not asking you to create an alternative reality. Instead, I'm asking you to stop fighting your reality by using it as fuel for your anger, resentment, and disappointment at not getting what you want. Embrace reality. Realize it's broken, messed up, and ugly. Recognize that it's put some internal and external consequences before you that will require effort to overcome. Seeing it for what it is will allow you to deal with it appropriately.

Joseph was born *on purpose* in this particular family. God did not make a mistake with the context of Joseph's birth. God allowed you to be born into your circumstance specifically. You were not positioned in your background accidentally. God wants to make your life a unique testimony of grace, one that is your unique story, one that will encourage and strengthen and help others around you. God wants you to own that story by his grace and not by your capacity. A part of finding your home in God is learning how to let go of your earthly baggage.

2. Lean in.

In churches, people get nervous the more they get to know each other. At our church, we have many small groups we call "life groups." We call them *life groups* because that's where life happens. That's where others can see past the veneer we showcase and perceive the unhealthy attitudes and actions that are present. That requires vulnerability. And being vulnerable is hard. We struggle with allowing others to take a closer look at our lives. We worry about what they might think.

At no point in Joseph's context are we told that anyone admitted to the sin that was happening. They didn't talk about how they felt or seek solutions. Resentments remained hidden. But just because something is invisible doesn't mean it's not there. Sin has a habit of making its way out into the open (Num. 32:23). As with a geyser, you'll never be sure when it will erupt.

Choose to name how you believe life has been unjust to you. The purpose is not to create resentment or anger. That already exists. The aim is to begin accepting where you are so that you can start following God from that context to something better.

3. Embrace your circumstances as the soil for your uniquely wonderful future.

Accept the good and the bad of your life, and then realize that these circumstances place opportunities before you that are unique to you. There's only one you. Your circumstances aren't there to punish you or hold you back. They are there, for better and worse, as the soil from which you can realize the potential in your future.

Those who've reached places of wholeness and healing don't disassociate from their backgrounds. Helen Keller didn't ask for illness. But her life became an inspiration, her voice amplified because of what she overcame. Losing to the Detroit Pistons is what ultimately moved the Chicago Bulls to overcome that obstacle to win their first championship. It wasn't a denial of losing. It was an embracing of that loss, in order that they might learn and grow from it.

Maybe you're marinating in hate, resentment, frustration, and resignation. But how is that working for you? Living with a fist raised to the sky when you look at the cards you've been dealt doesn't do anything to the sky or the cards. The truth is that not only can you learn to deal with the cards, the game itself can change. Rather than raising a fist to the sky, you can learn to lift your hands in praise. This is a process, but it's also possible.

And that begs a different question: How desperate are you for change? Embracing your circumstances allows you to begin navigating those circumstances. But that will require a change in your attitudes and actions.

Part One is the mess. Joseph was born into a mess. You were born into a mess. I was born into a mess. But are we condemned to it for the rest of our lives? No.

APPLICATION

God is creating a unique masterpiece through your mess. God has allowed you to be in the mess you're in so that he can work his grace to create a masterpiece.

1. Take some time to write down the mess you were born into.
2. What is some baggage that you may be carrying, or that you still haven't let go of?
3. Write down some grace transformations you hope to see.

2
It's Their Fault

"It wasn't me." —Shaggy & Rikrok

■

"But when his brothers saw that their father loved him more than all his brothers, they hated him and could not speak peacefully to him."
—Genesis 37:4

here's an annoying sound every parent with multiple children knows and dreads. It's the sound of blame coming from the backseat of the car. "He touched me! That's why I punched him." "She's calling me names! Make her stop." When I was a boy, my dad used to threaten to pull the car over and stop. The couple of occasions where I pressed to see if he would stop, I regretted it. I told myself I would never be that dad . . . until I had sons of my own. Suddenly, my father was so much wiser than I'd previously remembered. Blame gets wearisome.

What's the statute of limitations for blaming others for your life? I've heard people in their seventies blame their parents. I've heard people blame their bosses. I've heard people blame their animals. We're social creatures who are unbelievably broken. That brokenness rubs off on others and generates more mess.

Lee Strobel wrote, "I talked a few weeks ago with a lady who underwent physical abuse from her mom and dad who were deeply religious—they'd make her kneel by the bed and pray and then beat her." One of my grandfathers used to abuse his twin daughters after World War Two. One recounted being thrown out of the second floor of their house into the snow below one winter. The other recalled trying to hide the bruises when she went to school. A friend of mine used to hate Christmas because it meant both of his alcoholic parents were home. He and his sister used to hide in the closet while other kids were opening gifts.

"Have you ever been raped?!" yelled the angry nearly thirty-year-old man in front of me. He was contemplating suicide because his girlfriend had broken up with him. As someone who suffered from bipolar disorder, he was having an exceptionally difficult day emotionally. He'd stopped taking his medication. He was speaking from deep hurt (sexual abuse from a family friend), but this was also his trump card in arguments. I told him that while I hadn't, my wife had been sexually abused by a family friend. There are victims of abuse everywhere. So many can say, "Me too!" The truth is, some of what you're going through is, in fact, "their fault." You might blame your boss as your reason for hating your job, or you might blame your husband for your home life. Some blame their church, while others blame politicians.

Joseph's Brothers

Sometimes the bad guys are obvious. I like old Westerns because you know from the outset who the bad guys are. But in real life, it's not always that simple. Joseph's brothers wanted to kill him. They're the ones who sold Joseph into slavery. That makes them the bad guys. But it doesn't mean they're caricatures.

Joseph's father gave him a coat. He didn't help the situation. If there's another person to shoulder the blame, he would be the one. Sigmund Freud, of course, would likely agree because for him everything was a mommy or daddy issue. In truth, both Joseph's brothers and his father were fully responsible for their choices. Joseph bore the brunt of their decisions. "It's their fault!" he was sold into slavery. And it was.

Joseph went after his brothers and found them at Dothan. They saw him from afar, and before he came near to them, they conspired against him to kill him. They said to one another, "Here comes this dreamer. Come now, let us kill him and throw him into one of the pits. Then we will say that a fierce animal has devoured him, and we will see what will become of his dreams." But when Reuben heard it, he rescued him out of their hands, saying, "Let us not take his life." And Reuben said to them, "Shed no blood; throw him into this pit here in the wilderness, but do not lay a hand on him"—that he might rescue him out of their hand to restore him to his father. So, when Joseph came to his brothers, they stripped him of his robe, the robe of many colors that he wore. And they took him and threw him into a pit. The pit was empty; there was no water in it.

Then they sat down to eat. And looking up they saw a caravan of Ishmaelites coming from Gilead, with their camels bearing gum, balm, and myrrh, on their way to carry it down to Egypt. Then Judah said to his brothers, "What profit is it if we kill our brother and conceal his blood? Come, let us sell him to the Ishmaelites, and let not our hand be upon him, for he is our brother, our own flesh." And his brothers listened to him. Then Midianite traders passed by. And they drew Joseph up and lifted him out of the pit and sold him to the Ishmaelites for twenty shekels of silver. They took Joseph to Egypt.

When Reuben returned to the pit and saw that Joseph was not in the pit, he tore his clothes and returned to his brothers and said, "The boy is gone, and I, where shall I go?" Then they took Joseph's robe and slaughtered a goat and dipped the robe in the blood. And they sent the robe of many colors and brought it to their father and said, "This we have found; please identify whether it is your son's robe or not." And he identified it and said, "It is my son's robe. A fierce animal has devoured him. Joseph is without doubt torn to pieces." Then Jacob tore his garments and put sackcloth on his loins and mourned for his son many days. All his sons and all his daughters rose up to comfort him, but he refused to be comforted and said, "No, I shall go down to Sheol to my son, mourning." Thus, his father wept for him. Meanwhile, the Midianites had sold him in Egypt to Potiphar, an officer of Pharaoh, the captain of the guard. (Gen. 37:17b–36)

Dothan is an area of gently rolling hills that borders an ancient caravan route coming from Egypt. There were no natural springs in the region of Dothan, so over time, multiple water wells were dug. When one would dry out, someone dug another. A traveling caravan would have known some of those locations. Those who were herding in the area knew where to find water for themselves and their herds. Because of the undulating terrain, wells were not distinct. Some were full of water, and some were dry.

Eight of the eleven brothers wanted to kill Joseph. But Judah, the charismatic leader, had a different idea. He knew there were dry wells, and he knew about the caravans heading to Egypt. He was thinking, "win/win." How could they make a buck and also get rid of the "golden child"? Judah was looking for easy money. This was a selfish incentive, but it was also enough to rally his brothers to act smartly and selfishly. He suggested slavery and deceit. Dad wouldn't ask where they had gotten the money anyway. All they'd need would be a good alibi. And there was the added benefit that they wouldn't have to worry about disposing of the body.

Reuben, as the oldest, was trying not to rock the boat. He pretended to go along with his brothers because Reuben wasn't concerned with leadership, but appearances. His idea was to come back later, grab Joseph, and bring him home. Maybe Dad would be proud of him then. Reuben had a plan, but he didn't share it.

The author reminded us that while Joseph was a long way off, they saw him. Unfortunately, the English translation doesn't do justice to the expression "Here comes this dreamer." In Hebrew, it means "Here comes this master of dreams." Those of you who love and appreciate sarcasm will immediately hear the tone of this. "Here comes this so-called 'master of dreams.' Let's show him who's the boss!" Because the brothers had spotted Joseph a long way off, they had time to plan everything before he arrived at camp. They arranged an ambush.

Life is rarely two-dimensional. There are reasons Jacob and his other sons behaved the way they did. Perhaps a sibling in your life received a special gift (a car, help for college, a loan, or a special toy), and you didn't. That doesn't mean you sell them, pocket the money, and tell your parents they're dead. At least I hope not. What reasons pushed these brothers to the edge?

You likely don't want to read about those reasons. But this is one of those moments where I'm going to encourage you to look deeper. I'm not trying to torture you with details. Knowing why they behaved the way they did allows you to develop two critical things. The first is empathy. While Joseph's story is predominantly about his own journey, it's not *only* about his journey. That's an important distinction. Your life isn't only about you. Even as God is at work in your life, God is also at work in the lives of others. We have to make the deliberate choice to be as interested in those other participants as God is according to the story we've been given. If Scripture mentions the other brothers at length, it's doing so for good reasons. The second reason is hope. God will heal this family. This is not the end of the story of Joseph's brothers or his father. Once Joseph goes to Egypt, they drop out of Joseph's story for a while, but they'll return later.

In your life, you may look around you at those who deserve blame and think that ignoring them is the best policy. Because their individual stories don't excuse their actions or attitudes, you'll be tempted to believe that their stories don't matter. But they do. And ignoring them won't make them go away.

Joseph has ten older brothers and one younger brother. How those brothers related to their mothers, their father, and each other is particularly crucial to Joseph's story. Some of these names, because of their own spiritual journeys and their reactions to family dysfunction, will come up again later.

The Pack

Remember that this is an immigrant family. Jacob's sons had a pack mentality concerning their surroundings. In part, it was about a hierarchy of loyalty: family, then tribe, region, state, or country. Bottom line: if you lived in that area, you knew not to mess with Jacob's boys. The story of Shechem is one example.

There was a bloodbath in Shechem, and it involved the sons of Jacob. Remember that Jacob and his family were immigrants in the land of Canaan. And though the text doesn't list all of them, Jacob did not just have sons. He also had daughters. So, Joseph and his brothers had sisters. And sisters need to be protected.

Dinah was one of those sisters. In Genesis 34, Dinah traveled to Shechem to visit with some of the local women. The prince of Shechem, a man whose name was Shechem, "saw her . . . seized her and lay with her" (Gen. 34:2). Afterward, he fell in love with her. When Jacob found out about this, he waited for his sons. The prince was willing to do anything for Dinah.

His willingness is worth emphasizing because the brothers would use that motivation to get their revenge. They told Shechem that Dinah could never be married to an uncircumcised man. They made a deal that if every man in Shechem were circumcised, then the prince could take Dinah as his bride. And Shechem agreed! Every male picked the same day (emotional and physical support, I suppose) and did it together. It takes a while to heal from an experience like that, so the brothers waited until the men were good and sore, then swept in and killed them all. Their revenge scheme was smart but a low blow even by ancient standards.

If they faced outward, it was all for one. You messed with one person in the family, and you messed with all of them. And they weren't afraid to get down and dirty if they had to. But when they were by themselves, they worked against each other.

The Fractured Pack

Jacob lived in the land of his father's sojournings, in the land of Canaan. These are the generations of Jacob. Joseph, being seventeen years old, was pasturing the flock with his brothers. He was a boy with the sons of Bilhah and Zilpah, his father's wives. And Joseph brought a bad report of them to their father. Now Israel [Jacob also went by the name Israel] loved Joseph more than any other of his sons because he was the son of his old age. And he made him a robe of many colors. But when his brothers saw that their father loved him more than all his brothers, they hated him and could not speak peacefully to him. (Gen. 37:1–4)

From the outside looking in, they were one unit. But from the inside looking out, so much was desperately wrong. Here are the names of Joseph's brothers:

1. Reuben (Leah)	5. Dan (Bilhah)	9. Issachar (Leah)
2. Simeon (Leah)	6. Naphtali (Bilhah)	10. Zebulun (Leah)
3. Levi (Leah)	7. Gad (Zilpah)	11. Joseph (Rachel)
4. Judah (Leah)	8. Asher (Zilpah)	12. Benjamin (Rachel)

Anyone with siblings will tell you how influential they are to relational health. For a few years, my youngest son lived in terror of his older brother. My wife and I never knew. It had such a profound impact on his life that years later, he had a breakdown because of it. Childhood trauma can remain latent until it chooses to erupt.

Reuben

Reuben was the oldest son, and sons were a big deal. England's King Henry VIII killed for sons. Leah's first son was Reuben. Reuben's name meant *Behold, a son*. She named her oldest almost as a validation of her worth to Jacob. "Look, I've given you a son."

Reuben would have grown up knowing that his mother was desperate for her husband, his father, Jacob, to love her. All kids know things like that. And this would have been obvious. She probably told him to sit up straight, speak politely, and do well so that Jacob would see that he was her son and would choose to love her. Reuben was a reflection of the possibility of love for Leah. Reuben thought, *I have to be responsible enough and good enough. That way, Dad will look at me, be proud of me, and think better of Mom. Maybe he'll foster some love in his heart for her.* Reuben aspired to harmony and responsibility. Reuben did some bad things in private, but in front of his dad, he was continually trying to show Jacob that his mom and her son were both worth loving. He had one constant message. "Don't rock the boat!" Like many older children, Reuben was trying to prove to his father that he was a responsible man. But in private, he was broken.

Judah

Judah was Leah's fourth son. Leah's attitude shifted from seeking her husband's affection to God's love for her when she gave birth to Judah. "And she conceived again and bore a son and said, 'This time I will praise the LORD.' Therefore, she called his name Judah" (Gen. 29:35). Judah was also Mr. Charisma. Some middle children are like that. He didn't have the pressure that was on Reuben. He was the one about whom others thought, "Life just works out for Judah!" Judah had WOO. (WOO stands for "winning others over.") Judah was gifted at recruiting others to his ideas. Sadly, most of his ideas were selfish. As we read earlier, it was Judah who wanted to make a buck off of his brother. If Judah's name sounds familiar, it's because the promise of God would come through Judah. Jesus came from the tribe of Judah (Rev. 5:5).

Sons of the Handmaidens

Dan, Naphtali, Gad, and Asher were the sons of the handmaidens. The handmaidens were not on equal terms with Leah and Rachel, in terms of family hierarchy, because they were not Jacob's wives. So, there was a definite pecking order, with someone always trying to claw her way up the social ladder. These siblings knew and felt that tension. Thousands of years later you can almost still hear the teasing, insults, and fights that occurred among those brothers. It didn't mean there weren't happy times. But siblings can talk to one another in less than flattering terms. I only had one sister, and we knew exactly how to get under each other's skin as we were growing up.

Because of the spousal competition in the house, and because she couldn't bear children, Rachel had a conversation with her handmaiden. "Bilhah, please go sleep with my husband so we can have some more testosterone on our side of the team." And you thought your family had issues! Bilhah slept with Jacob, and together they had two sons, Dan and Naphtali. Leah heard about this and sent Zilpah to sleep with Jacob. Zilpah had a couple of boys by the name of Gad and Asher.

Just pause a moment and think of the months that roll by where someone in the house is pregnant, and someone else is doing the math to figure out which team is ahead on points. Now you're getting the idea of just how crazy this family dynamic is.

Joseph

Joseph was the oldest son of Rachel. Rachel was the only woman in the house who couldn't have kids. Her husband loved her most, and she couldn't give him children. She began weeping. God heard her prayers. Joseph was the result, the "golden child." He was the first son of his father's great love.

When Rachel gave birth to Joseph, her firstborn son, Jacob thought to himself, "Joseph, *you* are my favorite son." He played favorites, just like his father and mother before him. Just as his grandfather, Abraham, had played favorites. Parents sometimes do that.

The favoritism impacted Joseph's relationship with his siblings. All of his other brothers hated him. "But when his brothers saw that their father loved him more than all his brothers, they hated him and could not speak peacefully to him" (37:4). Twice more, in verses 5 and 8, the chapter repeats the fact that Joseph's brothers hated him.

To compound matters, Jacob was relationally clueless. Have you ever met somebody who relationally just doesn't have a clue what's happening? They think everything is going great, and you're at the table thinking, *Man, if you only knew what is happening right now.* It seems as if there's always one person at the table who is living with a delusion. They believe their daughter is a virgin, their son isn't smoking marijuana, and their wife isn't sleeping around. Everyone else seems to know but them! Cluelessness can be hurtful. Jacob was a clueless dad with no idea his other sons resented his preference for Joseph.

Dysfunction ignored is a broken merry-go-round. No one's sure what the other is doing, no one brings it up, and everyone just keeps going.

Sometimes people just go along. But going with the current can feed poor patterns of behavior. Some currents sweep us out into the ocean.

Jacob was so clueless, he must have thought to himself, *Do you know what I should do? I should give Joseph a special coat. Joseph, grab all of your brothers! Guys, you're going to be so happy for Joseph!* Color was a commodity in the ancient world. In effect, Jacob was telling Joseph's siblings that Joseph's clothes wouldn't be as drab as theirs because he was so precious. Jacob was just relationally clueless. If he'd had a relational clue, he probably wouldn't have continued to single out Joseph. But Jacob had his favorite, so he poured gas on the fire that had been quietly raging.

Others and You

It's foolish to think we aren't impacted by the decisions of others. And misery indeed does love company. But there's a difference between being invited to misery and accepting that invitation. Though the choices of others impact us, how we assign blame lies primarily within how we view self-efficacy. According to the American Psychological Association, "Self-efficacy refers to an individual's belief in his or her capacity to execute behaviors necessary to produce specific performance attainments. Self-efficacy reflects confidence in the ability to exert control over one's own motivation, behavior, and social environment." In plain terms, it's not about what others do to you. It's about how you view what is in your capacity to control.

Victor Frankl, a prisoner in a concentration camp, wrote an incredible book titled *Man's Search for Meaning*, on freedom despite being unable to control the actions of others. The title is telling because it's about how to find meaning when others try to determine your worth. He wrote, "No matter the circumstance, you always have the last of the human freedoms: to choose your attitude." You can choose to resent those around you, or you can choose a different response. Others bear the responsibility for their own actions and attitudes. You take responsibility for your own.

Your entire life will consist of the decisions of others encroaching on your path. God didn't create you to live in a vacuum, and he didn't create you to live with people who make no mistakes. At some point, you have to decide whether your legacy will consist of reactions or responses. The former will make you the ball in a pinball machine. Your trajectory will be determined by the pushes of others. The latter allows you a pathway to freedom. Miroslav Volf talked about soldiers targeting and killing his brother in the Eastern Bloc of the former USSR. His parents forgave the soldiers because "Christ forgave us." That didn't make forgiveness easy. But it did mean their actions weren't determined by the soldiers. They found freedom in Christ. When the Son sets you free, you are free indeed (John 8:36).

Lessons from The Blame Game

1. Don't give others the ability to manipulate your happiness.

Everyone in Joseph's family (except the clueless father) was obsessed with the family dynamic. "What does my brother think? What does my mom think? What does my aunt think? What does my uncle think? What's going on here?" The result was that happiness had been placed in the hands of others. In essence, they relinquished happiness by ceding who held control of it.

"My world will end if she/he doesn't . . ." is a sentence I hear a lot. It is manipulation wrapped up in longing. The person is either trying to manipulate the actions or attitudes of others or is being manipulated by them. Either way, manipulation isn't the same thing as love. It may get a person control. But control is a short-term stick of dynamite that will kaboom at any moment.

I'm so thankful that my parents', my spouse's, or my children's happiness isn't dependent on me. That would be a brick ton of pressure! Imagine someone coming up to you, demanding that you fulfill their longing for happiness. That is not only exhausting; it is also impossible. You can contribute to others' happiness, but you cannot satiate the hunger for it in others.

The source of your joy also cannot be you. You can't make yourself happy. What you can do is to change your expectations of who can do what in your life. You can stop living based on the approval and/or rejection of others. You must start thinking of living differently. What you can do this early in the process is to decide to uncouple the demands of others from your reactions to those demands.

2. Take ownership of your focus.

Your focus can't be on you. If it turns inward, the inevitable destination is selfishness and, ultimately, narcissism. You'll view everything around you through the perspective of how it impacts you. You'll find it difficult to celebrate the victories of others. You'll stop loving others for their own worth because you'll continuously translate everything back to your own sense of value. You'll love someone else because loving them makes you feel good. That isn't love, but self-gratification.

Taking ownership of your focus is not pie-in-the-sky advice. It's imminently practical. It requires discipline. And it's genuinely difficult. If you were to begin a business based on the reactions of everyone around you, you wouldn't be able to get it off the ground, because the nature of the company would change based on the whims of others. This doesn't mean you ignore others, either. But it does mean you are relentlessly focused on why your business exists. If you want to ride a bicycle, don't look down at the wheels or stand at a balance. Instead, fix your eyes on a point out in front of you and start pedaling toward it. Of course, anyone who has learned to ride a bicycle knows that bicycle riding is easier in retrospect than it is at the moment. At the moment, it means having the courage to potentially fall down. But the promise of the ride is worth the risk.

Everything else will spring from your focus. It's about what you do, every day, to keep your focus on God. You might receive a text message that eats away at your thoughts or have someone push your buttons (those select buttons we all have that irritates us) and fall at first. The key is to remember that those buttons are being pushed because they can be. Instead of focusing on what was done to you to make you so irritated, you need to refocus. Don't blame others for your lack of focus.

Take ownership and look out in front of you. That's the only way you'll ever learn to ride.

Joseph's family sounds like a lot of Christian families. So many live on the premise of Jesus and all he's done for them. Their proof is in their activities. Kids are enrolled in church programs and they attend church regularly. They have the mantras and rituals down pat. But apart from Sunday mornings, they're not seeking God in their daily choices, attitudes, or actions. When everything blows up, they wonder why. They seek God and enlist prayer. When God answers, they go right back to their previous pattern. Jesus isn't Lord over their lives. Jesus is a fire extinguisher in the form of a person. No fire, no need to use the extinguisher. And yet, the house keeps burning down.

The Bible talks a lot about the importance of the search. When we are determined and persistent in seeking God, we are promised that we will find him. That is a seeking in the ups and downs. It's about the persistence of focus. Because God loves you, he gives you the free will to choose to focus on whatever or whomever you like. But just because something is permissible, it doesn't make it advisable. Instead of riding the rollercoaster of faith, you will need to focus on the One upon whom your faith should rest. God, not others, must become true north.

3. Practice empathy.

Empathy is the ability to understand and share the feelings of another. You don't have to carry the other's feelings with you wherever you go. But it does help to see where they're coming from. For example, if a mother abuses her children because she was abused as a child, this does not excuse her behavior. But it does allow you to see her in a light that sheds some understanding. You can detach the value of the action from the value of the person. To have empathy, you have to see beyond yourself and how the other person impacts you.

Steven Covey stated, "Most people do not listen with the intent to understand; they listen with the intent to reply." He shared a story on the principle of empathetic listening in his book *The 7 Habits of Highly Effective People*. "I was in a quiet subway car when a father and several children boarded. The children were running wild, bothering passengers so much I asked the parent if he could rein them in.

"Oh, you're right. I guess I should do something about it," the distraught father replied. "We just came from the hospital where their mother died about an hour ago. I don't know what to think, and I guess they don't know how to handle it either."

This doesn't change the fact that the man's children were running wild and bothering passengers. But it does provide context to their behavior. Context allows us to understand and then seek out responses based on that understanding. When we understand what's happening and why, we have a higher likelihood of finding a different response. Sometimes, the gateway from reaction to response is empathetic listening. Someone is trying to push your buttons to get you to react not solely because they're trying to make you miserable, but because they want you to be as miserable as they are. And that takes them from a two-dimensional antagonist to a three-dimensional broken person. Sometimes, that little shift makes all the difference.

APPLICATION

1. What percentage of your suffering would you place on your circumstances?

2. What percentage would you place on the people in your life?

3. How do you react externally and internally when others "push your buttons"?

4. Who do you find it most difficult to have empathy for? In what ways can it be easier to reduce someone from a person to a caricature? If someone is a caricature, how do you find healing with him/her if you're not a caricature?

Maybe Some of This Is Me

"If stupidity got us into this mess, then why can't it get us out?"
—*Will Rogers*

■

*"But when his brothers saw that their father loved him more than all his
brothers, they hated him and could not speak peacefully to him."*
—*Genesis 37:4*

After we've blamed our circumstances and the people around us,
there's a nagging question we have to answer: Am I the problem?

In the early twentieth century, *The London Times* ran a series
of newspaper articles answering the question "What's Wrong with the
World Today?" To generate interest, they asked famous figures to write an
essay answering the question. Each week they would publish a different
piece. One renowned writer they invited to contribute was a Christian
named G. K. Chesterton. "What's wrong with the world today?" He
famously wrote, "Dear Sir, I am. Yours, G. K. Chesterton." Anyone who
has frustrated themselves knows this to be self-evident. Sometimes, we're
the problem.

The Bible teaches, "The good person out of the good treasure of his
heart produces good, and the evil person out of his evil treasure produces
evil, for out of the abundance of the heart his mouth speaks" (Lk. 6:45).
But what happens when your heart is lying to you? What happens when

you long to be good but behave poorly? Self-reflection should lead us to align longing with action. But many spend their lives avoiding that kind of introspection. That's why people typically need help from a therapist. They need a guide to confront them. The narcissist rarely admits to narcissism.

Most struggle to put a full period at the end of the sentence, "I was wrong." Instead, we punctuate with commas: "I was wrong, but you" or "I was wrong, but they" or "I was wrong, but I had no choice." We absolve ourselves from being complicit in our messes.

We all contribute to the messes in which we're born. Sometimes the problem isn't the world. Sometimes the problem is us. A boy cheats on his math test and then wonders how he wound up grounded by his parents and in detention. An unmarried teenaged couple has sex and then are surprised to discover the woman is pregnant. Plans get altered forever. A worker steals from his employer by being lazy and finds himself laid off. Words spoken in anger in arguments cause weeks, months, or sometimes even years of heartache and require even longer to repair.

One day, mom and I discovered that dad had had extramarital affairs. I was a pre-teen. Up until that point I was convinced Dad had all of the answers to life and faith. But on that day, I watched as the mess he'd created required clean-up everywhere around him. I'll never forget the day Dad told me, "The sin is my own. Please don't confuse my sin with the God I serve."

We moved to Northern California. For a while, we weren't sure if Mom and Dad were heading for a divorce. It was as if an asteroid had fallen on our world and destroyed life, and when life came back into view, nothing was ever the same. When I was a freshman, I was so angry at my father that I challenged him to a fistfight on our front lawn. I wasn't just mad. I wanted to break something. In other words, I wanted to start a mess of my own.

I could spend my life blaming my father, but at some point, the problem was me. I allowed my anger to dictate my responses. Maybe some of the mess I experienced was me. I wasn't at fault for my father's infidelities, but I was responsible for how I responded to my father afterward.

The distinction between what happens to you and how you choose to respond to it is crucial. It's the difference between adding layers to the complexity of a situation or turning it around to find peace. Counselors work hard with clients to uncover the why's of the client's attitudes and actions in life. But discovering the why is half the work. The other half is changing the what, who, when, and how. Placing blame on circumstances or on other people partially explains why you behave the way you do. What it doesn't do is excuse that behavior. There were other options for you to choose.

Erwin McManus once tried to illustrate how we sometimes blame God for consequences that are a result of our decisions and not his. He brought someone up onto the stage and gave him a tennis ball. He told the person to throw the ball at a wall. Erwin didn't specify which wall, which angle, or how hard to throw the ball. The person threw the ball, and to his surprise, it bounced back and hit him! The audience erupted with laughter. The person said, "Why did you make me do that?!" Erwin replied with all of the things he didn't tell him (wall, speed, angle) and then asked why the person was surprised that when he threw the ball at the wall, it bounced back at him. His point was that sometimes actions have reactions. They have natural consequences. Throw a ball at a wall, and it will (likely) bounce back at you. Yet so many blame God when the ball bounces back! The mess isn't the result of God's intervention. Sometimes, the consequences are the result of our sinful actions.

After dad had some sessions in counseling, his steps grew lighter. Why, I wondered, wasn't he as burdened as before? His response was that he'd finally traced his insecurities to his childhood. He knew why he sought fulfillment through the admiration and attraction of others. But once he knew that, he now faced the equally difficult challenge of taking responsibility for expressing that why with attitudes and actions he had chosen that were relationally damaging not just to himself, but also to others. At some point, your why is an excuse, not an answer.

How Joseph Contributed to His Own Mess

If you've ever been singled out and alienated, you know it. In Joseph's family, Joseph felt estranged from his brothers. He was isolated because he was his dad's favorite son, and because of his dad's relational cluelessness. His alienation stemmed from the tension between his mother and his aunt(s). As a result, Joseph longed for others to recognize his significance. That's Joseph's why. Here's what Joseph did and how he did it, because Joseph also contributed to his alienation.

> Joseph, being seventeen years old, was pasturing the flock with his brothers. He was a boy with the sons of Bilhah and Zilpah, his father's wives. And Joseph brought a bad report of them to their father. (Gen. 37:2)

The storyteller wanted us to know how old Joseph was at this point. This is an odd detail. Perhaps it's because the storyteller wished us to understand the chronology. Or maybe there's something more. Perhaps the storyteller wanted the reader to know that Joseph was old enough to be relationally aware. Joseph was old enough to be emotionally healthy. Joseph was no longer a boy. He was old enough to make good choices. He was seventeen years old. The sons of Bilhah and Zilpah were Dan (Bilhah), Naphtali (Bilhah), Gad (Zilpah), and Asher (Zilpah). You'll recall that they weren't the oldest or youngest sons but had been born firmly in the middle.

The storyteller doesn't tell us what the "bad" report regarded. The reader is left to wonder, did these four brothers born of these two handmaidens deserve a bad report? We don't know, but the answer is "probably." There's a good chance that his brothers were doing something they shouldn't have been doing when they were all out taking care of the herds.

Perhaps the question isn't about what they did. For the storyteller, that is not pertinent. The real curiosity is, how was that report told? Why and how did Joseph share that report with his dad? The text doesn't explicitly say it, but it implies that Joseph related it in a way that didn't help his own alienation. He told it in such a way that contributed to his alienation from his brothers. In other words, Joseph's reputation in the house over the last seventeen years probably hadn't been one full of encouragement and grace. Joseph was *not* known as the encourager of the bunch. He wasn't doing himself any favors.

Joseph knew of his isolation within his own family, and within himself he had a massive longing for significance. He probably thought, *Dad and Mom love me, but my brothers don't seem to. I'm alone and isolated and by myself and more than a little bit insecure as a result. But I can't shake this sense that God has something more for me. One day, they'll see that I was born for greatness!*

Dreams would be a prominent part of Joseph's life, and these dreams encouraged Joseph in the dark moments of his childhood. God was telling him he wasn't alone. Joseph had no friends, and God was offering hope in Joseph's loneliness. But in his insecurity, Joseph perhaps thought, *Hey, I should share these dreams with my family!* And then he did.

> Now Joseph had a dream, and when he told it to his brothers, they hated him even more. He said to them, "Hear this dream that I have dreamed: Behold, we were binding sheaves in the field, and behold, my sheaf arose and stood upright. And behold, your sheaves gathered around it and bowed down to my sheaf." His brothers said to him, "Are you indeed to reign over us? Or are you indeed to rule over us?" So, they hated him even more for his dreams and for his words. Then he dreamed another dream and told it to his brothers. . . . But when he told it to his father and to his brothers, his father rebuked him and said to him, "What is this dream that you have dreamed? Shall I and your mother and your brothers indeed come to bow ourselves to the ground before you?" And his brothers were jealous of him, but his father kept the saying in mind. (Gen. 37:5–11)

Joseph felt an innate need to share these dreams with the same brothers who already found him annoying and arrogant. And Joseph wasn't looking for an interpretation. Everybody knew what he was saying. They all knew what these dreams meant. Nobody was saying, "What a coincidence! Wow, eleven sheaves and your sheaf stood upright. I wonder, who could that be? We should spend some time discussing this dream. Oh, man! Joseph's dreams are tough to figure out." Joseph demonstrated a lack of discernment.

Jacob, Joseph's father, understood the kind of dreams that came from God. Remember, this was the same Jacob who had had a God-sent dream in Genesis 28 of a ladder that reached to heaven. When Joseph said he had a dream, his dad would have known how that felt. He would have known what it was like to have God himself provide hope in the midst of despair. What did Jacob do? He rebuked Joseph for sharing!

The one person who Joseph thought would always support him said, "The sun, the moon, and the eleven stars are going to bow down to you? You're telling me that this whole family, myself included, should revere you because your ego destines you for greatness. Son, that's arrogant. You're trying a little bit too hard." Jacob thought Joseph's sharing was arrogant (and he was the one adult who *liked* him!).

Now his brothers went to pasture their father's flock near Shechem. . . . And he said to him, "Go now, see if it is well with your brothers and with the flock, and bring me word." So, he sent him from the Valley of Hebron, and he came to Shechem. And a man found him wandering in the fields. And the man asked him, "What are you seeking?" "I am seeking my brothers," he said. "Tell me, please, where they are pasturing the flock." And the man said, "They have gone away, for I heard them say, 'Let us go to Dothan.'" So, Joseph went after his brothers and found them at Dothan.

Shechem was a place fraught with danger. It was a place you didn't want to journey to alone. Joseph decided to wear his ornamental coat of many colors on his journey to visit his brothers there. Joseph contributed to this mess. Not only had he given a bad report of his brothers and demonstrated a lack of discernment in what he was sharing and how he was sharing it, but also he now decided, "You know what? I should wear this gaudy coat when I go check up on my brothers in Shechem." He didn't take a travel coat. He didn't wear a mantel that would help him blend in. Instead, he took the one that made him stand out.

There's an old story of a ship's captain who is sailing along one day, looking for enemy ships. His shipmate comes up and says, "Hey, captain, we just spotted an enemy vessel on the horizon." The captain says, "How many are there?" He says, "Just one." He looks at him and says, "Get me my red shirt." The shipmate says, "Why?" He says, "Because when we engage in the battle, I want the men to be inspired. If I take a cut or a bullet or something and I bleed, they won't see the blood because of the red shirt, and they'll be inspired and fight on." So, the two ships engage in the battle, and his frigate wins this battle. About a week later, they're out looking again for the enemy, and the shipmate comes up to the captain and says, "Captain, I've spotted enemy vessels." He says, "Wonderful. How many are there?" He says, "Seventeen." He turns to the shipmate and says, "Get me my brown pants."

Joseph was clueless and vain, and those traits led him to draw a giant bullseye on himself. The text says Joseph's brothers saw him while Joseph was far off. Of course, they did! Joseph was colorful. He was easy to spot. They saw him coming and started talking with each other, "Here comes this dreamer. Come now, let us kill him and throw him into one of the pits."

Earlier, we examined how our actions can create unforeseen reactions. Throw the ball against the wall, and it might just come back to hit you. The action was that Joseph chose to wander around Dothan in a coat that made him easy to spot. In the process, he unwittingly reminded his brothers why they hated him so much. The reaction was that, because of his coat, his brothers planned to kill him.

They saw him from afar, and before he came near to them, they conspired against him to kill him. They said to one another, "Here comes this dreamer. Come now, let us kill him and throw him into one of the pits. Then we will say that a fierce animal has devoured him, and we will see what will become of his dreams." But when Reuben heard it, he rescued him out of their hands, saying, "Let us not take his life." And Reuben said to them, "Shed no blood; throw him into this pit here in the wilderness, but do not lay a hand on him"—that he might rescue him out of their hand to restore him to his father. So when Joseph came to his brothers, they stripped him of his robe, the robe of many colors that he wore. And they took him and threw him into a pit. (Gen. 37:18–24a)

Then they took Joseph's robe and slaughtered a goat and dipped the robe in the blood. And they sent the robe of many colors and brought it to their father and said, "This we have found; please identify whether it is your son's robe or not." And he identified it and said, "It is my son's robe. . . ." Thus, his father wept for him. Meanwhile, the Midianites had sold him in Egypt to Potiphar, an officer of Pharaoh, the captain of the guard. (Gen. 37:31–36)

There's a small detail we sometimes overlook in this story. Joseph's brothers needed to convince their dad that their brother was dead. They didn't want to be called out as liars, in the event things went poorly, so they needed Jacob himself to come to that conclusion. They took Joseph's coat of many colors and dipped it in just one color, red. At that point, the coat was only a one-colored coat. It was no longer unique. When they showed Jacob, he recognized it by something else other than color. He probably knew the pattern and cut. Joseph's brothers were making a symbolic statement. "Joseph is no better than we are. His coat is just the same as ours." Joseph sent his brothers a signal by wearing the coat to Dothan. Joseph wanted others to recognize his significance. His brothers sent a message by dipping it in blood. "Joseph, you're just as significant as we are, except we're here and you're in slavery."

Sometimes God gives us unexpected gifts, and we slowly turn snooty. If we're not careful, we can begin looking down at others and signaling,

"Look at what God is doing with me." We cease communicating humility and start behaving arrogantly. Those around us would love nothing more than to take our coats of many colors and reduce them back down to one color.

Be careful with the signals you're sending to other people. People will either listen, ignore, or act against you. Sometimes they do so as a reaction to the decisions you make. Most of what we communicate is non-verbal. What are you saying, and why?

Taking Responsibility

Switchfoot sings a lyric saying, "Where can you run to escape from yourself?" Ultimately, you can't. It is one thing to have a psychological challenge. It is another to blame your life on that challenge. "It wasn't me. It was the [*insert your psychological condition here*] that caused me to do it." We're separating ourselves from our conditions, which can be good (we are not our sins), and bad (we are, in fact, sinful!). A person behaves poorly toward another and then blames their poor behavior on personal traumas. They say, "It wasn't me, but my dysfunction." It may be true that the poor behavior sometimes flows from trauma, but understanding why is different from excusing the act. The son of an abuser need not use his trauma to abuse his own son.

Albert Schweizer once wrote, "Man is a clever animal who behaves like an imbecile." While that's something we believe about others (politicians, governments, and everyone else we believe is to blame), it's not something we like to believe about ourselves. Schweizer expanded, "Man must cease attributing his problems to his environment and learn again to exercise his will—his personal responsibility in the realm of faith and morals." Philosopher Jean-Paul Sartre noted that a condition of our freedom is that we bear responsibility for what we do with it. "Man is condemned to be free; because once thrown into the world, he is responsible for everything he does." We're not as trapped as we think we are, and everyone around us isn't fully to blame for our responses.

Often, we read stories like Joseph's and we think we know who to blame. In these opening chapters, the obvious culprits appear to be his brothers. I'm not saying that Joseph "had it coming." He didn't deserve to be sold into slavery, betrayed by the family who knew and resented him. But Joseph wasn't completely innocent either. Joseph bore responsibility for those things he could control.

Lessons from Joseph's Contribution to His Mess

1. Your why may explain the conditions or motives for poor attitudes and actions, but they are not an excuse for them.

When the Eagles made a comeback album they named it *Hell Freezes Over*. The first single on the radio was a song called "Get Over It." I know what you're thinking: *If only it were that easy*. It's not. That said, the point of the song resonates for a reason. At some point, you have to stop using your past as an excuse for your present. Where to begin? Exactly there: by declaring your past will no longer be your excuse for your current choices. You have to choose to take personal responsibility for your life. Are there other factors at work? Yes, there are. Is your past a ball and chain? Yes, it can be. But making progress is different from standing still or going in circles. Twelve-step programs all start with an admission to others. What those who made that admission will tell you is that it's only partially an admission of guilt to those in the group. It's also an admission to oneself. Personal responsibility begins with humility. Humility requires courage.

We can't always change our circumstances or those who've wronged us, but we can improve our responses. Your life will either be an inspiration or a warning. Now and again, I'll hear someone say, "I have no regrets because my mistakes made me the person I am today." That answer sounds noble at first blush. But think deeper. You've never made a mistake you wish you hadn't? And you became the person you are today by doing whatever you wanted? Pay attention to the way you respond. Here are some things I believe the future Joseph would have told his younger self:

Use language that builds others up. Joseph wasn't known as the encourager of the bunch, yet God uniquely positioned him to encourage his brothers. He was the one son who could build bridges across his complex family dynamics. Joseph was special. He was the oldest son of the woman his father loved most. Imagine how meaningful an encouraging word from Joseph might have been. "Listen, brothers, I can't do anything about the way Dad views me. I know I'm his favorite, but you matter. We're in this together. We're brothers. Reuben, I just want you to know what a great job you do as the oldest. I'm following your lead. You're an inspiration. You watch over me. Judah, you're amazing. You have all this natural leadership ability. How about we channel that to something good for a change?" Choose conversations that build others up.

Significance is demonstrated, not demanded. Joseph wasn't the leader in the group. He couldn't even get a brother to like him, let alone follow him. How do you know you're a leader? If someone is following you. Joseph looked behind him; no one was there. And yet Joseph was so desperate for significance and influence that he shared dreams of how others would bow down to him. He demanded an audience. That was a mistake. The future Joseph would have gone back and said, "Listen, younger Joseph, if you want to be significant, you have to start being the kind of person others would want to follow."

Exercise discernment in the signals you're sending. Joseph could have left the multicolored coat in his closet on occasion. He didn't need to wear it everywhere, and certainly not on a long and potentially dangerous journey. But his decision to wear that coat communicated something particular about himself to others. The truth is that what you choose to wear (physically and metaphorically) says something about you. What are you saying?

2. Be careful what you long for.

Many of us have master plans for our lives forged by secret longings. Typically, they fall into three categories. First, we long for admiration. Some use Botox, while others go shopping. On Facebook and Instagram, we try to project our lives as a Pinterest image of inspiration for others. I've known of couples on the brink of divorce who posted smiling, magazine-quality pictures up until the date the paperwork was signed. The era of celebrity and fame has many aspiring for beauty. And we want it in high definition.

The longing for admiration can lead to emotional neediness. The outworking is a desperation for constant validation of worth. The individual wants everything they say or do affirmed, and that leads to a serious challenge of loving someone enough to help them by not affirming them when they're wrong. There's an inward cyclone that begins to twirl, where the individual is seeking worth, but knows that not everything they do is worthwhile. They need, but actually don't want, someone who can affirm their worth without approving of every action or attitude exhibited. This is a cyclone leading to a Mariana Trench at the bottom of which lies a fragile ego.

Second, we long for influence, typically in the form of wealth. In our social dialogue, we talk about the "disease of poverty." Poverty is something we avoid. Poor people are associated with unimportant people.

I grew up in the 1980s, an era of yuppies and opulent wealth, portrayed by Gordon Gekko in the movie *Wall Street*. In a famous speech from that film, Gekko declared, "Greed is good." In a survey from Pew Research a few years ago, the number one aspiration of Generation Y (also known as the Millennials) was "to be rich." Wall Street holds the American economy hostage. It seems everyone wants to afford another vacation, clothing item, car, boat, or house.

I meet people all the time who are looking for a platform of influence. They yearn for others to listen to them, based on their own need for authority. As one person told me, "I think I have the gift of criticism. People should listen to me before they start something." They want people to do what they say. But sadly, many are not willing to put the work into their character that matters for significance.

This longing for influence can lead to a lack of morality or healthy focus. The individual pursues items that can never satisfy, and there is someone more influential just ahead of them. The actor longs to be a director who longs to be a producer who longs to be a movie executive

. . . who in turn longs to be an actor. Be careful of what you chase. You may wind up catching it.

Third, we long for security. The master plan of many is summed up by the saying "Don't rock the boat." Our society is living through an anxiety epidemic. Tim Elmore wrote in *Generation Z Unfiltered*: "This generation of children and teens suffer from more mental health problems than any other generation of kids in American history. Both secondary schools and colleges report an insufficient number of counselors available to serve the students seeking help on campus." A recent *New York Times* article headlined, "People Are Taking Emotional Support Animals Everywhere. States Are Cracking down." For many, a master plan includes security for themselves, family, and friends.

The challenge is that life is unpredictable. Children need parents who do not panic in a crisis. Friends need others who bring perspective and hope. Ultimately, the individual finds ways to retreat from life rather than to embrace life. The circle of the person they could become shrinks to the size of their fears, and the courage needed to overcome them grows with each passing year.

APPLICATION

1. Describe ways you've contributed to your mess.
2. Write down a prayer to God accepting personal responsibility.
3. Take some time to be honest about your responses to circumstances so far. What signals are you sending to others about your longings? What are some things you can change to align your actions or attitudes with Jesus?

The Mess Good Choices Can Bring

"I can resist everything except temptation." —Oscar Wilde

∎

"And as she spoke to Joseph day after day, he would not listen to her, to lie beside her or to be with her." (Gen. 39:10)

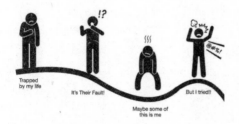

An alcoholic decides to stop drinking, so on the first night of sobriety he sits at the bar and sips water. Instead of applauding him, his drinking buddies decide he's no fun anymore. The alcoholic loses his friends for making the right choice. We see this pattern repeated over and over. The gossip stops gossiping and loses their friends. The accountant catches some questionable entries and instead of receiving a promotion is let go from their position. The overweight person goes on a diet and is applauded for the effort, but no one wants to have dinner with them anymore.

Change isn't just hard, it also has consequences. When you disrupt the status quo, the landscape alters. Sometimes, doing the right thing brings consequences that are confusing and discouraging and adversely impact your life. We might even ask ourselves, "Why try? What's the point? I want my life to be better, not worse." Every disruption, every learning curve, has moments where the attempts seem unworthy of the effort, not because of us, but because of the reaction to our efforts.

Unknowingly, we sometimes step into dynamics that can cause damage to our careers or reputations because we step into the immoral behaviors of others. What happens when a person trying to do the *right* thing meets someone bent on doing their *own* thing?

Joseph Does the Right Thing

Now Joseph had been brought down to Egypt, and Potiphar, an officer of Pharaoh, the captain of the guard, an Egyptian, had bought him from the Ishmaelites who had brought him down there. . . . So Joseph found favor in his sight and attended him, and he made him overseer of his house and put him in charge of all that he had. . . . [T]he LORD blessed the Egyptian's house for Joseph's sake; the blessing of the LORD was on all that he had, in house and field. So he left all that he had in Joseph's charge, and because of him, he had no concern about anything but the food he ate. (Gen. 39:1–6)

Joseph was sold into slavery and then purchased by Pharaoh's captain of the guard, a man named Potiphar. He was a foreigner in Egyptian culture. He had to learn the language, customs, and expectations of his master . . . fast. But Joseph was also smart and determined. He rose through the ranks of Potiphar's house to become the chief slave. Potiphar trusted him more and more. With every new area of trust, Joseph excelled. The spoiled son showed there was much more to him than met the eye. In other words, Joseph had time to think about how he'd contributed to his mess, and he adjusted. Remember Joseph's why? He longed for others to recognize his significance. This time, Joseph decided not to demand significance, but to serve others well. This is an important shift in the expression of his insecurity and longing. How did he do that?

For the first time in Joseph's story, we see Joseph's leadership potential. We're often told that the best leaders have two kinds of intelligence: emotional quotient (EQ) and intelligence quotient (IQ). EQ helps us navigate our world socially, while IQ helps us process and apply information appropriately. Joseph had EQ and IQ. He could relate to and lead others (EQ), and he was intelligent (IQ).

How did Joseph develop his emotional intelligence? He was in a position where he had to serve. Joseph clearly served *well*. But in jobs that deal with people, completing the task is half the equation. The other half is working as a part of a team. Joseph clearly worked well with others. Working well with others often requires excellent communication and empathy skills. Joseph was a leader. As one expert on leadership commented, "You know you're a leader if you turn around and people are actually following." Note that Joseph was likely not Potiphar's first slave. The other servants already there followed him. There was no uproar or resentment that Joseph was promoted as the leader of the servants. And he was quickly promoted.

Leadership is usually extended, not demanded. Potiphar was a leader himself. As a leader, he understood the importance of finding good people he could trust and empower with responsibility. The text tells us Potiphar completely trusted Joseph with the parts of his life that were closest to him personally. Joseph shared a sense of stewarding that responsibility, because of his concern for Potiphar's trust when he was tempted to break trust.

Joseph had a sense of humility. He could not demand promotion, nor could he dress in such a way that his possessions contributed to his status in the house. Why? Because Joseph didn't own anything! Joseph had gone from favored son to slave. His reaction to his new situation was to accept responsibility for a better attitude.

Joseph also had integrity. He didn't cheat or berate others. Joseph wasn't mean or lazy. Potiphar realized he'd hit the employee jackpot. Joseph became the person in charge of "all that [Potiphar] had" (Gen. 39:4). Why? The text states, "because of [Joseph] [Potiphar] had no concern about anything but the food he ate" (39:6). Joseph took Potiphar's concerns away, so Potiphar didn't need to worry about his home life.

The immediate result was that Joseph experienced a blessing in the midst of his circumstances. Joseph was focused and determined and moving up! Life wasn't easy, but it was less chaotic than his previous life.

The movie *Zoolander* (2001) is a comedy about a model named Derek Zoolander. In it, we're told that Zoolander can't help the fact that he's "really, really, really ridiculously good-looking." That's the kind of description made of Queen Esther, the girl who won the Miss Universe Pageant in the book of Esther. The Bible tells us that in addition to being smart, being a great leader, and having integrity, Joseph was "handsome in form." To put it in modern terms, he had Brad Pitt's abs, George Clooney's chin, and Denzel Washington's smile. He was handsome in appearance.

I'm a little jealous of the Bible's description of Joseph. I was kind of hoping he'd have some hidden defect. He was smart *and* good-looking. Unfair! Have you ever seen a star athlete who seems to have it all? Guys like Joe Montana, Aaron Rogers, or Tom Brady, and then thought to yourself, *Yeah, but I'll bet he's miserable in other ways.* We love to bring others down to our misery. It's not enough that they might actually be happy. We hope they've got something wrong with them so we can feel confident they are as average as the rest of us.

Joseph seemed to be in a positive place in life. But what happens when a healthy person meets someone else's unhealthy world? Misery loves company.

Now Joseph was handsome in form and appearance. And after a time, his master's wife cast her eyes on Joseph and said, "Lie with me." But he refused and said to his master's wife, "Behold, because of me, my master has no concern about anything in the house, and he has put everything that he has in my charge. He is not greater in this house than I am, nor has he kept back anything from me except you because you are his wife. How then can I do this great wickedness and sin against God?" And as she spoke to Joseph day after day, he would not listen to her, to lie beside her or to be with her.

But one day, when he went into the house to do his work, and none of the men of the house was there in the house, she caught him by his garment, saying, "Lie with me." But he left his garment in her hand and fled and got out of the house. And as soon as she saw that he had left his garment in her hand and had fled out of the house, she called to the men of her household and said to them, "See, he has brought among us a Hebrew to laugh at us. He came in to me to lie with me, and I cried out with a loud voice. And as soon as he heard that I lifted up my voice and cried out, he left his garment beside me and fled and got out of the house." Then she laid up his garment by her until his master came home, and she told him the same story. . . . As soon as his master heard the words that his wife spoke to him, "This is the way your servant treated me," his anger was kindled. (Gen. 39:6–19)

Potiphar's Wife: Bent on Doing Her Own Thing

The reader has no idea what's going on in Potiphar's marriage. We're left to speculate. Was Potiphar abusive or an absentee husband? Was his wife bored? What was their marriage dynamic to make her so obsessive to bed Joseph? All we know as the reader is that theirs wasn't a healthy marriage. Married people simply didn't sleep around in that culture. Or if they did, it was rarely the wives. The wives were considered the property of their husbands. This does not mean that they didn't have dignity or self-volition. Lest we forget, Cleopatra was Egyptian. She wasn't weak. Women of that day still had self-respect. Many had self-volition. But they didn't have much in the way of power. A woman had everything to lose if she slept with someone else. Potiphar's wife isn't even given a proper name for the reader to know her. I'd love to call her something other than Potiphar's wife. But we're not given her name. We're told to whom she was married. She belonged to her husband. This doesn't mean that people didn't fall in love or marry for love. But the typical mindset of marriage was about belonging *to* someone rather than joining together toward a broader pursuit. Joseph alludes to as much when he states that Potiphar "kept" her (Gen. 39:9).

Potiphar's job title put him in proximity with the man Egyptian culture believed was a god (Pharaoh). And Potiphar wasn't just any guard. He was "captain of the guard." That meant that Potiphar's wife probably lived in luxury. Because of Joseph, all Potiphar had to worry about was work and "the food he ate." The Bible isn't being figurative here. It's being literal.

Potiphar's wife was upper class. The goal of the upper crust was to be in a position where they did not have to work. The aspiration and value for work is a relatively late development in history. That's not to say work wasn't appreciated. It's always been appreciated. But the goal of the wealthy was to not labor. It was a mark of status when you were in a position where others worked for you, and you could spend your day pursuing leisure. Think *Jane Austen*. There were a lot of bored, wealthy people engaging in social standing.

We also see that Potiphar's wife wasn't running the house. In fact, she doesn't appear even to want to run the house. Maybe she was busy having afternoon tea with other upper-class wives. Notice what was happening:

Chasing Joseph took time. "And after a time, his master's wife cast her eyes on Joseph and said, 'Lie with me'" (Gen. 39:7). This was not an overnight temptation. Yes, Joseph was attractive in appearance. But Potiphar's wife didn't start lusting immediately. Potiphar's wife was not always trying to cheat on her husband. "After a time" means that her cheating may not have been an ongoing issue. Potiphar's wife was likely not sleeping around with many people. Something was unhealthy in their marriage. Their relationship was functional . . . until it was dysfunctional. It was working until Potiphar's wife thought the solution to her own longings was to sleep with Joseph. She wanted to do what she wanted to do, whether it was the right thing to do or not. From her perspective, sleeping with Joseph was a way to find happiness.

Potiphar's wife was not cavalier. Her efforts to sleep with Joseph were not something to be laughed at. When Joseph ran away, she called in the "men of her household" (39:14) to say that Joseph was after her. She was a woman scorned, and she made up a story re-casting herself as the victim. But what she wasn't cavalier about was her efforts. Were she cavalier, she might have laughed and said, "Oh, I tried, and he ran, but he has to come back at some point!" A knowing smile might have crept across her face as she played this game of cat and mouse with Joseph yet once more. But she didn't do that. She knew that what she was doing was dangerous. She was deliberately betraying her husband's trust. She knew what was at stake. When Joseph ran, she knew she had to get ahead of the damage by re-framing the narrative.

She kept trying. "And as she spoke to Joseph day after day, he would not listen to her, to lie beside her or to be with her." Potiphar's wife kept trying. Joseph kept refusing. Day after day. Temptation after temptation. Or maybe she was gorgeous. Perhaps it was a severe temptation for Joseph. Whenever my wife and I conduct pre-marital counseling, we remind the couple that "the wolf is always at the door." The truth is that at some point in a marriage, there will be attractive opportunities to stray. We don't know if it was difficult to refuse from the perspective of Joseph (maybe Potiphar's wife wasn't appealing to him). Perhaps it wasn't much of a temptation. But what we do know is that Potiphar's wife was persistent. And not just persistent, she was insistent. She took things to a new level when one day, she "caught him by the garment."

Potiphar's wife was like Visa. She was "everywhere he wanted to be." Joseph had to deal with the challenge of proximity. He fled. He did the right than stroke his ego (i.e., he could bed the wife of his boss) he remembered his significance wasn't found in her arms.

The Garment Caught

But no one can run forever. Eventually, having done the right thing, Joseph had to return to the house. By that time, Potiphar's wife had made up a story that cast her as the victim. It was likely that all of the servants knew she was lying, but who was going to speak up?

When your boss tells you to lie to a client, and he then re-casts you as the villain of the story because you didn't, who in the office will speak up when they know the truth? Everyone is too busy saving their own skin. And that's what happened to Joseph. The other slaves knew better than to cross Potiphar's wife.

In a perfect world, this story would have a different ending. It could have been the first story of a sexual harassment lawsuit in Egypt. Or maybe Potiphar might have investigated his wife's claims and found Joseph innocent. Maybe Potiphar's wife would have gotten the message that Joseph wasn't interested and simply tempted someone else. She could have become someone else's problem. But we don't live in a perfect world. In the real world, everyone's sin sloshes all over everyone else around them. What are we to do?

Let me give a plain answer to the temptation question. When temptation comes, and the odds are stacked against us in an unfair world, do the right thing anyway. I know that's not a popular answer. The popular answer is, "Do what society or the circumstance tells you. Do what you can get away with." Society tends to change its mind fast. What was once accepted becomes anathema. Let me encourage you to choose the timeless option. Do what is right, regardless.

Doing what was right landed Joseph in prison. But God's long-term plans for Joseph were better than Joseph could imagine. Doing what is right isn't easy. But your best life is always in alignment with God's will.

Sleeping with another man's wife isn't right. Tempting another person into sexual sin isn't right. Trying your best to sway a partner to do something they don't want to (but you do) isn't the godly approach. Prepare yourself to accept the consequences for good choices.

Joseph had no idea how his story would turn out, but he made choices according to God's standards anyway. All Joseph could do at the moment was to trust and obey. And hope.

Hope is powerful. "And we know that for those who love God, all things work together for good, for those who are called according to his purpose" (Rom. 8:28). But for all things to work together, the subsequent verses remind us that it is God himself who has to be our justice. We are to look like people who are conformed to the image of his Son, and that is no small thing when we recognize how unfairly Jesus was treated. At times, you may be mistreated for making good choices. But don't let that stop you from making them.

Jesus made perfect choices. He was crucified because of them. Those who would seek to destroy us by those good choices forget that our power lies not in our strength, but in our submission to God. In that sense, the world is not battling us. They are fighting God's standards. God's biblical standards exist so that we might be made "complete" and "equipped for every good work" (2 Tim. 3:17).

Lessons When Good Choices Reap Bad Consequences

1. Determine your response to temptation.

Temptation has a sense of timing. Have you ever noticed that just when we're determined to do what's best, temptation comes along? Just think about how committed you were to fulfill your New Year's resolutions. How long did it take for temptations to decrease your resolve? A lure works because it's attractive to us. Temptation sidles up to our ego and tells us that we can "do what we want to do." We believe the lie that God will be okay with whatever we want to do. But were God not to care about anything we want to do, he would be apathetic, not loving. Adam and Eve were tempted to eat what they weren't supposed to eat. Their sons, Cain and Abel, had offerings God told them to give. Thinking that God didn't care about sheep or produce, Cain was tempted to offer something less than his best. The temptation to do what we want is always knocking at our door.

Sometimes, temptation happens in small ways. I love pastries. One of my extra-biblical beliefs is that when I get to heaven, there will be a German (or French) bakery where carbs don't convert to sugars. I can't find that heavenly bakery in the Bible, but I'm still looking.

Pastries in moderation are okay. But eating cakes when you're trying to be fit and healthy isn't helpful. I don't care how much you reshape broccoli; it will never be as appealing as donuts for me. Just when I decide to drop a few pounds and get healthy, someone brings donuts into the office. It's as if temptation knows when I'm watching my waistline and sends donuts at that moment. When I'm most determined, attraction to a lesser choice seems to be right there to challenge me. The days when I'm not on a diet, there's not a donut for miles around.

That's just one small way that lesser things try to pull us away from the things we know we're supposed to do. On the scale of donuts, it's a relatively small struggle (big for me, but maybe small for you). But what happens when we scale up the temptation? On the scale of extra-marital affairs, it's devastating.

Sometimes temptation grabs you by the metaphorical "garment." Your boss asks you to lie to a client. Your friend asks you to help them cheat on a test. Your lawyer tells you how to cheat on your taxes. There's always something at stake; usually, it's a relationship. If you don't lie, your boss won't promote you. In fact, he or she may even fire you. Your friend says you're not a real friend because real friends help others pass their tests by cheating. We've all been there. Sometimes, no matter what you choose, it seems like a lose/lose proposition.

But you never know. The truth is that as we stand in those ethical junctures, we don't see the outcome. Our imaginations start working overtime to fill in what we think may or may not happen. We might actually garner greater trust by doing the right thing. Or we might find ourselves in a weaker position by doing the right thing. We simply don't know at the time we face the choice.

My dad and mom had different approaches to playing card games. They had two favorites: Rook and Pinochle. Each of those games involves partnering with someone across the table. You have bids on the points you think you can make, then a specific color or suit is declared, and the partners work against the other players to make their bid. "Talking across the table" is a phrase used to describe someone trying to tell their partner which cards they have without getting caught.

For mom, "talking across the table" was the best part of playing cards. She would find all kinds of creative ways to cheat. She would howl with laughter if caught. And if she wasn't caught, then she would howl with laughter after they won and point out how she cheated. For her, cheating at cards was a part of the fun of the game. It wasn't serious.

For dad, "talking across the table" was cheating, pure and simple. He was going to win fair and square, or he refused to play. Dad took his cards seriously. For him, it was a reflection of character. When Mom and Dad played together, she would talk, and he would turn red with frustration. They loved each other but did not make great card partners. Card partners should behave with the same set of values on the game, but life isn't like that.

Temptation also lies to us. Billy Joel wrote and sang a catchy song titled, "Only the Good Die Young." In it, he's a boy trying to convince a girl to sleep with him. He sings, "Come out, come out, come out, Virginia, don't let me wait." Temptation always tries to justify itself. In this case, Billy Joel is telling Virginia that she's going to give up her virginity at some point, so it might as well be to him. If we're not careful, we can fall into a similar line of thinking. Fate means we have no choice; something will ultimately "happen" with someone. We think it's better if we do the lying, cheating, or stealing rather than someone else. Oddly, it's the same kind of hubris that often has us flirting with temptation. We want to be close enough to tell ourselves we're tough, but far enough away to resist. Of course, it rarely works out that way.

Hubris tells us we're tough enough. If not Joseph, then perhaps someone else who won't treat Potiphar's wife with nearly as much dignity and respect. "I might as well be the one." But that's a lie for two reasons. First, it assumes that fate trumps a free will. It is free will that leads to *choosing* love. You have a choice. You're not destined to blow it. Second, it implies that you're a better option than the next candidate for sin. You convince yourself that it's better for the other to cheat with a "nice person" than a "bad person." Scripture tells us to submit and flee because we're not strong enough. When you know you aren't strong enough, humility becomes the entry point for honesty. Honesty tells you to get out of the room because you just don't know how you might respond.

You might be thinking that the best people in life never experience temptation. You're thinking, *Maybe temptation is targeting me because I'm weak.* But you'd be wrong. Jesus was perfect, and he was tempted (Lk. 4:1–13). If he wasn't immune to temptation, why are we surprised when it comes? What surprises most isn't *that* temptation exists, but *when* it arises. We're shocked to discover that temptation has a sense of timing. And that timing typically sabotages something good.

James 4:7 says, "Submit yourselves therefore to God. Resist the devil, and he will flee from you." When the enemy attacks, we resist by standing and persevering. Not all attacks by the enemy are temptations. So, what do we do when the enemy tempts rather than attacks us?

The biblical principle to apply when you're wondering how to respond is to *resist* the devil and *flee* temptation. When temptation comes your way, the answer isn't to do what you think you should do. In Galatians 5:16–17, the apostle Paul instructs us, "But I say, walk by the Spirit, and you will not gratify the desires of the flesh. For the desires of the flesh are against the Spirit, and the desires of the Spirit are against the flesh, for these are opposed to each other, to keep you from doing the things you want to do." Temptations are ego strokes, telling you to worship idols like money, fame, reputation, etc. They puff you up to begin bragging or complaining. They lie to you by telling you that you'll find happiness through someone or something stroking your fragile ego. James reminds us, "But each person is tempted when he is lured and enticed by his own desire" (1:14).

When we submit to what God says, we have rules and ethics outside of ourselves to inform our responses. There's a distinction between what I want to do and what the Bible tells me to do. My submission to God determines my choice. I don't pursue what I want, no matter how afraid I am of the outcome or how good it may make me appear.

In Jesus's temptation, the embodiment of truth (Jesus) met the universe's greatest liar (Satan). Should Jesus have resisted or fled? His answer was both. Jesus spoke Scripture against the devil. So, he resisted. But he also fled. One way of fleeing temptation is to remove yourself from the question and allow Scripture to remind you that God is the One who is in charge of your ego. Jesus effectively told the devil, "I'm not going to engage you with what I think. My ego is being tempted. Here is what God the Father says through Scripture. Hear it for yourself." Scripture can cut through the noise and confusion in our lives. Scriptures are both your refuge and your revelation. They shelter you from your ego, and they reveal things as they really are.

It helps that the Bible has specific things to say on particular types of temptations. Sexual temptations have always been a part of the human story. For example, Samson was tempted by Delilah. There were sexual temptations in the early church. Sexual sins span human history, so it is no wonder that sexuality is addressed so explicitly in the Bible. Paul writes, "Flee from sexual immorality. Every other sin a person commits is outside the body, but the sexually immoral person sins against his own body" (1 Cor. 6:18). Paul's point here is that the temptation is to think the sin resides with the other person. "She or he tempted me," so if I cave, the crime rests on the other. What the Bible reminds us of is that when you give yourself sexually to someone else inappropriately, you're stealing from yourself. So, you're adding a complication on top of a temptation.

Matthew writes, "Watch and pray that you may not enter into temptation. The spirit indeed is willing, but the flesh is weak" (Matt. 26:41). Sexual temptation is one of those sins where proximity isn't helpful. Any teenage boy and girl left alone know that proximity and isolation are a terrible combination. Sexual immorality (especially before the age of the internet) required proximity. The challenge we face in the age of the internet is that we've narrowed proximity and still expect purity. We need safeguards to help us with the latter when the former can't be avoided. It's why we need help fleeing temptation. The flesh is weak. When we're standing in front of those doors alone and in the cover of darkness, it's too easy to open doors we shouldn't.

2. Good choices, despite bad consequences, train your identity.

Joseph made a choice to flee temptation and suffer the consequences of false accusations. In doing so, he learned that his identity was not grounded in his job position. What was God doing? He was training Joseph away from personal insecurity. Joseph made a seminal choice that his allegiance to God would determine his life actions. It was the first time that Joseph made a decision that wasn't based on what he would receive but on the righteousness of God. Righteousness means "living rightly." Joseph chose to live rightly for its own sake.

Earlier, we saw that when Joseph shared his dreams, it was all about his search for acceptance and value by his brothers and his father. When Joseph wore his coat to visit his brothers, it was all about feeling important. When Joseph chose to serve, it was about stopping the pattern of seeking attention. But as he sat in a prison cell, he was no longer burdened with the need for others to affirm his acceptance or value. He no longer had Potiphar to affirm his worth. God was reshaping Joseph's need for affirmation from others. Joseph's right response to temptation was also an opportunity for Joseph to choose personal validation from God.

How does an insecure person become a confident person? By learning to place his or her confidence in someone higher than their instincts, rationale, or feelings. Some people overcorrect and become arrogant or cocky. But arrogance or cockiness is actually born from insecurity. Why? Because we know the truth about ourselves. We understand how deeply flawed we actually are. It is when we reap adverse consequences for good choices that God is moving our locus of affirmation away from others to himself.

3. Good choices, despite bad consequences, build resistance.

Dr. Manuel Rauchholz tells the story of seeing a coconut tree in a greenhouse. The coconut tree was held upright by wires. Having seen thousands of coconut trees in his life, Dr. Rauchholz was astonished. He had never seen a coconut tree that required wires to remain upright. Inquiring why they were needed, someone explained that the root system had not developed properly. Why hadn't it developed? Because the greenhouse blocked winds from blowing against the tree. Because of breezes, gusts, and wind exposure over time, the trees build up resilience by developing root systems to withstand the adversity. Over time, coconut trees can withstand hurricane-force winds and still stand.

When I look back on my life, I'm glad I didn't always know what lay ahead. The choices I once perceived as mountains, were in retrospect molehills. That doesn't minimize the mountain you're facing. The mountain you're facing is still your mountain at this time. But it is to say persistence through adversity is built up by facing adversity over and over again. When hurricanes come, our tree will either stand or fall.

Jesus uses the example of building your house on a rock or on the sand. His point is to have a foundation built on Jesus as the cornerstone and the bedrock of Scriptures.

> Everyone then who hears these words of mine and does them will be like a wise man who built his house on the rock. And the rain fell, and the floods came, and the winds blew and beat on that house, but it did not fall, because it had been founded on the rock. And everyone who hears these words of mine and does not do them will be like a foolish man who built his house on the sand. And the rain fell, and the floods came, and the winds blew and beat against that house, and it fell, and great was the fall of it. (Matt. 7:24–27)

Jesus's point is that it's in acting on God's instructions that resilience is developed. God sends us choices that may ostracize, hurt, or wound us if we choose what he wants. But none of it is pointless. God uses it all to build a character of courage.

The road to God's horizon is rarely straightforward. When we trust God through the twists and turns on this road of life, choice by choice, we are placing our future in his hands. We are telling God that we will not give lip service to faith, but we will walk by faith. "Now faith is the assurance of things hoped for, the conviction of things not seen" (Heb. 11:1). The consequences we face are the consequences of faith in God.

Will you live to do what feels good or will you live based on what God says is right? The answer won't necessarily be learned quickly. Remember: The godly choice is always best. Run if you have to. Resist when you must. Submit to God's standards at all times.

APPLICATION

1. Think of ways you've been tempted in the past. How have you been tempted? How have you been the tempter?

2. How have you been held hostage by resentment or bitterness at something unfairly spoken about you or done to you? What can you apply from the lesson of Potiphar's wife and Joseph's response, in order to let resentment or bitterness go?

3. We all have regrets. There are things we've done that we wish we hadn't done. How can you put your sorrows in the rearview mirror of your life? What do you need to confess to God or put down so that you are not a person marked by regrets?

4. Write down your top three most difficult moral choices below. Write down what the Bible has to say about the core ethics those choices may require (honesty, integrity, peace, wisdom, joy, etc.). Finally, write down what you think might happen if you reap adverse consequences for the right choice. Now take a black marker and mark out column three. Ultimately, remember you are only responsible for columns one and two. Take some time to pray through those responses. Enlist prayer support from others as you make godly choices.

my difficult moral choices	God's core ethics	what might happen

Letting Go

"Hope is being able to see that there is light despite all of the darkness."
—Desmond Tutu

∎

"So he asked Pharaoh's officers who were with him in custody in his master's house, 'Why are your faces downcast today?'" —Genesis 40:7

A doctor says to his patient, "I have bad news and worse news." "Oh dear, what's the bad news?" asks the patient. The doctor replies, "You only have twenty-four hours to live." "That's terrible," said the patient. "How can the news possibly be worse?" The doctor replies, "I've been trying to contact you since yesterday."

Murphy's Law states: If something can go wrong, it will. A variation of that law is: Smile. Tomorrow it will be worse.

Sometimes things go from bad to worse. *The Washington Post* reported on the story of a man who was told he had leukemia. After an experimental treatment, he seemed to have beaten the odds. The doctors were thrilled. Then, inexplicably, the man's health rapidly became much worse. Sandra Boodman wrote, "He became moody, confused, and delusional — even childish — a jarring contrast with the even-keeled, highly competent person he had been. He developed tremors in his arms, had trouble walking, and became incontinent." The doctors thought he had a rapid form of dementia. As in an episode from the television series *House*, the doctors struggled to make a diagnosis. Sometimes when we think things can't get any worse, they do.

A marriage slowly implodes, and then the bottom drops out because of a revealed affair. A student is shunned from their friends at school and then is handed an "F" on a paper. A prodigal spends his inheritance and finds himself feeding pigs with none of his so-called friends around to give him a hand. I once took my car in for an oil change and two hours later walked away with a bill for $1,000 for other things that they found wrong with the vehicle. Just when things seem low, they can still get worse. We wonder, where is God in those moments?

In *The Hiding Place*, Corrie ten Boom recalled a story and a prayer from her sister Betsie regarding fleas in their concentration camp barracks. She wrote:

"Betsie, there's no way even God can make me grateful for a flea."
"Give thanks in all circumstances," she quoted. "It doesn't say, 'in pleasant circumstances.' Fleas are part of this place where God has put us."
And so, we stood between piers of bunks and gave thanks for fleas. But this time I was sure Betsie was wrong."

As the story unfolded, the guards wouldn't enter the barracks—which allowed the prisoners to read their Bibles and have small prayer gatherings—because of the fleas. The fleas, which seemed a curse, turned out to be a blessing. Low points are like that.

At some point, you'll reach a low point. It is at this place that no one and nothing else is blamed, you see yourself as you are, and your insecurities grow tired of manifestation. It is a dark, often desolate, place. But it is not without purpose.

Joseph's Low Points

Some time after this, the cupbearer of the king of Egypt and his baker committed an offense against their lord the king of Egypt.

And Pharaoh was angry with his two officers, the chief cupbearer and the chief baker, and he put them in custody in the house of the captain of the guard, in the prison where Joseph was confined. The captain of the guard appointed Joseph to be with them, and he attended them. They continued for some time in custody. (Gen. 40:1–4)

By the time we arrive at Chapter 40, Joseph is twenty-eight years old, having languished in prison for quite a while. "Some time after this" means that his time in jail leading up to the time he turned twenty-eight was substantial. The episode with Potiphar's wife put Joseph into a prison designed for the political prisoners and servants Pharaoh despised (literally, the place where "the king's prisoners were confined"). It was a hole intended for enemies of the state.

Joseph spent the prime years of his life there. Some estimate he spent eleven years in prison. Though Joseph was in charge of all the prisoners in jail, things were still bad; it was like being the lead rat on a sinking ship. Joseph went from being the chief slave for Potiphar to the servant of the king's prisoners (Gen. 40:4).

One day an angry Pharaoh threw two more prisoners in the hole for Joseph to serve. "The captain of the guard appointed Joseph to be with them, and he attended them. They continued for some time in custody." This moment is the lowest point of Joseph's story. Joseph is about to hit rock bottom, so we should read and understand this section carefully.

And one night they both dreamed—the cupbearer and the baker of the king of Egypt, who were confined in the prison—each his own dream, and each dream with its own interpretation. When Joseph came to them in the morning, he saw that they were troubled. So he asked Pharaoh's officers who were with him in custody in his master's house, "Why are your faces downcast today?" They said to him, "We have had dreams, and there is no one to interpret them." And Joseph said to them, "Do not interpretations belong to God? Please tell them to me." So, the chief cupbearer told his dream to Joseph. . . . When the chief baker saw that the interpretation was favorable, he said to Joseph, "I also had a dream." (Gen. 40:5–16)

The Chief Cupbearer and The Chief Baker

It's helpful to know who these two pivotal prisoners were because they broke Joseph's heart. One prisoner was the chief cupbearer. In the book of Nehemiah, we're told that Nehemiah was "cupbearer to the king" (Neh. 1:11). The cupbearer's role was to taste the food and wine before the king ate and drank. The cupbearer placed the cup in Pharaoh's hand (Gen. 40:21). He was the last line of the king's defense in case of an attempted assassination by poisoning. This position required someone expendable and someone trusted, like being the lead butler on Downton Abbey. Cupbearers took pride in their position, and because the cupbearer's own life was on the line, he would take extra precautions to ensure that the food and drink weren't poisoned. In the story of Joseph, the cupbearer was a good guy and was no fool.

The chief baker was an opportunist. He baked for Pharaoh, but he did something more than present a burnt croissant to the king. We aren't sure exactly what he did, but from his interaction with Joseph and his dream, his character was questionable. When Joseph interpreted the cupbearer's vision, the baker shared his dream when he saw "the [cupbearer's] interpretation was favorable." He saw an opportunity for a good outcome in his predicament.

Bible commentator K. A. Mathews made a keen observation about the baker's dream. In it, "the baker is totally passive." He wanted to see which way the wind blew and then jumped in that direction. The baker wasn't someone acting with moral integrity. Instead, his moral position likely depended on the situation.

"One night, they both dreamed" (Gen. 40:5). God was doing something supernatural here because there are similarities between the two dreams. Both men were disturbed by dreams that occurred on the same evening. If you've ever woken up with a sense of dread, this was one of those mornings. These dreams were vivid and confusing, and this only added to the men's fear and concern. They were spooked, and Joseph noticed.

Divine interventions are relationships and connections God provides providentially. First, these two men were in a dark place, literally. Prison isn't exactly a happy place. It is often a dark, dank place. Second, they were despondent. Joseph had experienced hopelessness and despair. Joseph could relate.

Whenever we bear witness to the grace and power of God, it's incredible how often our circumstances align alongside those of other people on the journey of life. Not ahead of or behind, but *next* to you. It's in seeing different reactions to the same difficult circumstances that conversations tend to begin with earnestness and honesty.

Though the two men shared similar dreams and circumstances, there was a difference in their character. Be careful of assuming that a dark place will lead others to a character change. In the story of the prodigal son, the younger son made a series of poor decisions. When he reaped the consequences of those decisions, he determined to go back to his father. The father met him in an embrace even as the prodigal was making his way home. I meet many Christians who share the hope that a friend or family member will have the same experience. "When you're down, the only way to look is up" is the rationale.

But in life, that is only partially true. *Some* face upward. Others keep looking down and simply transfer their lousy character traits over to their new situation. These people will continue to use others and seek ways forward on their own power. That's the case with the baker. The baker wasn't reflective or honest; he was opportunistic and presumptuous. Some of the people we encounter in the dark places of life will be like the baker.

Others will be like the cupbearer. These are people who have good intentions but address their interests first. He was probably a man of integrity, but he also had a survival instinct. That made him smart, but not necessarily one to risk his neck for someone else unless there was a good chance he'd come through it alive. The cupbearer wasn't looking out for himself, but he was also not cavalier about how helping others might impact his own life.

Neither man's name is provided. Yet they aren't in the story as a simple segue into Joseph's transition to prominence. The cupbearer was a man of consequence. Why? Sometimes God brings people into your life who aren't there to be your friends in the dark places but are there to help you grow through the dark spots. These are people who will come in and out of your life, people you may attend to, a teacher, a classmate, or an acquaintance. That's the case with Joseph.

Fata Morgana

A Fata Morgana is an illusion, a trick of the eye. It's a mirage. Sailors look out on the horizon, and objects or landmasses can appear to float. As you drive your car on a hot day, a Fata Morgana makes it appear as if the road ahead is breaking up into the sun. In the desert, a Fata Morgana is the illusion of water when there is none.

Joseph saw a Fata Morgana. After interpreting the dreams of the cupbearer and baker, Joseph had one request, "Only remember me, when it is well with you, and please do me the kindness to mention me to Pharaoh, and so get me out of this house" (Gen. 40:14). The cupbearer agreed and then forgot for two years. Forgetfulness is something to which all of us can relate. It's usually unintentional and harmless.

An elderly husband and wife visit their doctor when they begin forgetting little things. Their doctor tells them that many people find it useful to write themselves little notes. When they get home, the wife says, "Dear, will you please go to the kitchen and get me a dish of ice cream? And maybe write that down so you won't forget?" "Nonsense," says the husband, "I can remember a dish of ice cream." "Well," says the wife, "I'd also like some strawberries and whipped cream on it." "My memory's not all that bad," says the husband. "No problem—a dish of ice cream with strawberries and whipped cream. I don't need to write it down." He goes into the kitchen; his wife hears pots and pans banging around. The husband finally emerges from the kitchen and presents his wife with a plate of bacon and eggs. She looks at the plate and asks, "Hey, where's the toast I asked for?"

We were talking about this passage with the teaching staff at our church when one of our pastors said, "There's more than one way to forget. Sometimes it's intentional." That's the likely scenario in the Joseph story. Restored to his position, the last thing he wanted to do was to draw attention to himself in unnecessary ways. His thought was simple: *Keep your head down and get to work.* Pharaoh had been upset with him once, and so the cupbearer did everything in his power not to rock the boat. He remembered Joseph, but Joseph was intentionally "forgotten" for the sake of personal survival. The result was that Joseph languished another *two* years in prison. What were you doing two years ago? When you think about it, that's a long time.

For 730 days, or twenty-four months, Joseph lived with the knowledge that he had helped someone, had asked them for help in return, and then heard nothing. I'm sure that when he asked the cupbearer to remember him, the cupbearer smiled and nodded. Joseph likely replayed their conversation dozens of times and wondered if there was a non-verbal clue missed. Had he misjudged the man's character? For a short moment, Joseph had his hopes up. "The cupbearer promised he would put in a good word for me. He can get me out."

The distance between expectations and reality is the level of disappointment. What makes a prison worse? The possibility of hope that never arrives. Just when it seemed things couldn't get any worse for Joseph, they did. Joseph was forgotten yet again. His inner longing for others to notice his significance was ground down until there was no trace left. What was God doing? What was his purpose for having Joseph in this position?

Lessons About Letting Dysfunction Go

1. At the bottom, God teaches us to be his regardless of who's paying attention.

So many people put conditions on God. "I'll follow you if," "I'll love you if," "I'll believe in you if," "I'll be faithful to you if . . ." But God can't be leveraged. God is God, and you and I are not God. We are not all-knowing, all-powerful, or all-present. We can leverage nothing with a God who has it all. The whole idea of putting conditions on obedience is insulting to God. God wants you and me to love him simply because we love him—without conditions and with loving hearts.

Joseph once dreamt of significance. God was removing Joseph from the center of Joseph's dreams so that God could be at the center. Joseph's brothers took away his coat, but God was taking away Joseph's ego. Instead of being self-centric, Joseph was learning through reliance, humility, and circumstances how to be God-centric.

Joseph learned to serve at the bottom of life. At the darkest place in his story, he brought God into the fore. He embraced service and humility before God. A humble person is willing to help without praise or applause. When we learn to serve simply for the sake of helping, we begin to change.

Jesus spoke about that kind of service in Matthew 20:26–27, "But whoever would be great among you must be your servant, and whoever would be first among you must be your slave, even as the Son of Man came not to be served but to serve, and to give his life as a ransom for many." Joseph responded the way a servant of God responds. In the darkest places of life, Joseph learned to respond with grace. Genesis 40:4 reminds us that Joseph *"attended them . . . for some time."* Joseph had been consistently serving the king's prisoners without receiving anything in return. In the darkest places, God is teaching us how to give without receiving.

2. God uses the dark places in life to help us become fully aware.

God was increasing Joseph's empathy. In dysfunctional families or relationships, there's often a lack of understanding for the other person. As a boy, Joseph wasn't exactly empathetic. As a young man, Joseph likely grew in empathy for his team of coworkers. But at the bottom, we read the following, "When Joseph came to them in the morning, he saw that they were troubled. . . . *Why are your faces downcast today?*" (Gen. 40:6–7). Joseph both noticed how these two prisoners were feeling *and* asked them about their emotional state. And he was genuine about it. He didn't ask them so they could ask him how he was doing. People do that sometimes. They're not interested, but they feign interest so that the concern comes back in their direction. But Joseph was genuinely concerned. Joseph had to get to the end of himself to be in a place where he would start tending to others.

God was teaching Joseph understanding. Joseph had had dreams in the past, but he'd stopped dreaming. Up to this point in his life, Joseph had never interpreted the dreams of others. This was a uniquely divine moment, and Joseph recognized the hand of God at work. "Do not interpretations belong to God? Please tell [your dreams] to me" (Gen. 40:8).

Isn't it interesting that God developed understanding and empathy in the context of relationships? So often, we interpret the darkest places in our lives as being inherently about us. We retreat into ourselves. But often, it is in the tough moments that God calls us to step outside of ourselves to care for others. Change comes in the context of relationships—of our relationship with God and our responses to others.

Joseph understood that God gave dreams. In this case, he gave dreams to others. Joseph was not the dreamer in this part of the story. Sometimes I'll use someone else's circumstances to draw parallels to my own. There's nothing wrong with that because we all relate to each other with shared experiences. But there's a subtle temptation to turn the conversation toward our own experiences or feelings if we're not careful. We can make the conversation about us instead of the other person. Joseph didn't talk to the cupbearer or baker about his history with dreams. Instead, he wanted to serve them by helping them understand God's dreams.

3. God uses the dark places in life to help us become relationally assured.

God was teaching Joseph discernment. Notice how Joseph approached the cupbearer and baker. In Genesis 40:8, he said, "*Please* tell me." Later, in verse 14, the phrasing of his request to the cupbearer continued to be remarkably polite. Joseph did not demand. He didn't step into a divine moment with an air of self-importance. There was no flair or flurry of activity associated with his interpretations. His was a simple, humble conversation.

But it was also discerning. Joseph asked the cupbearer to remember him because Joseph was hoping for justice. In verse 15 he stated, "For I was indeed stolen out of the land of the Hebrews, and here also I have done nothing that they should put me into the pit." His request was one that let the cupbearer know he hoped for justice. Joseph asked for an innocent man to be set free. Why is that discerning? I believe the cupbearer was innocently caught up by Pharaoh's anger. In Gen. 41:10, he recounted, "When the Pharaoh was angry with his servants and put me and the chief baker in custody in the house of the captain of the guard." This makes Joseph's request a discerning request. Joseph was saying, *We're both innocent. Please remember what it's like to be accused and in prison for something you didn't do. And let Pharaoh know about it so he can right a wrong.*

The Dark Night of the Soul

St. John of the Cross famously wrote of a common Christian experience for those growing in spiritual maturity. He described what he called a "dark night of the soul":

> At a certain point in the spiritual journey, God will draw a person from the beginning stage to a more advanced stage. . . . Such souls will likely experience what is called "the dark night of the soul." The "dark night" is when those persons lose all pleasure that they once experienced in their devotional life. This happens because God wants to purify them and move them on to greater heights. . . . God perceives the imperfections within us, and because of his love, urges us to grow up. His love is not content to leave us in our weakness, and for this reason he takes us into a dark night. He weans us from all of the pleasures by giving us dry times and inward darkness. In doing so he is able to take away all these vices and create virtues within us. . . . No soul will ever grow deep in the spiritual life unless God works passively in that soul by means of the dark night.

Genesis 40 was Joseph's dark night. But it was never without purpose. "After two whole years" of Joseph's languishing in prison after the incident with the cupbearer and baker, Pharaoh would have a dream. One small phrase for *two years* of a dark night of the soul. But in that dark night, God was reminding Joseph that he was in control of the timing. God alone knew the destination. God had not given up on Joseph.

When we reach bottom in life, our first impulse is to blame God. We assume he doesn't care about us. We shake our fists at the sky. We weep under the covers of our blankets, asking him why he's forgotten us. We blame God instead of honoring God.

My friend Raimund and I met in Austria. When we became friends, Raimund was very bitter at God. His brother had died of cancer a couple of years previously. A Christian group in the area had told him that God had the power to heal his brother. They all prayed over the brother. His brother died. After his death, some Christians said to him that God had the power to raise the dead to life. They prayed for God to do just that. His brother didn't come back to life. So Raimund came to two conclusions. First, if there was a God, then God didn't care about him or his family. Second, if there was a God, then that God would do whatever he wanted to do regardless of what others asked from him. As a result, Raimund walked away from exploring faith in God. He blamed God for not answering the fervent prayers of his followers. He blamed God for the death of his brother.

In Psalm 42, the psalmist is in a depressed place in life. And yet, in the thick of it, the psalmist asks and answers his own desperate situation, "Why are you cast down, O my soul, and why are you in turmoil within me? Hope in God" (v. 5a). The least becomes the greatest because they embrace hope. When hope is rooted in God alone, we become rooted as people, regardless of our circumstances.

You might be in your own dark night. You might be asking yourself how things have gone from bad to worse. You may be at the bottom. Let me encourage you: God has a purpose for the bottom. Don't forget that God is showing you steadfast love in the midst of the darkness. It may not feel that way, but I promise you, his love is there. God can use the bottom to turn you toward him. He did it with a prodigal son. He did it with Jonah in the belly of a whale. He did it on a bloody cross on a hill described as "the place of the skull." There is no chapter 41 without chapter 40. God is in control of the trip, and the journey is worthwhile. I promise.

My mom suffered from a disease that ravaged her body year after year. When I was born, she was 5'7" tall. When she graduated to heaven in 2009, she was 4'11". Mom had an incredible voice and was a lead vocalist in her school in Germany. God allowed her neck and back vertebrae to fuse together. Mom was a multi-instrumentalist. She played the piano, violin, and accordion. God allowed her hands to deform and the bones within them to disintegrate. Mom loved to hike. The pain in her feet grew so bad and deformed she used a walker, feet braces, or someone's shoulder. That shoulder was often mine. One year, one of her legs had to be amputated just below the knee. Mom knew about dark places. When things got bad, it seemed they could always get worse.

And yet, mom had more joy in her sickness than I did in my health. She made life fun. What do you do when you love to sing, and you can't turn your head? You sing anyway. Mom not only led church choirs but also turned our family into the von Trapps. I grew up singing four-part harmony. When my voice changed, mom simply switched my part to bass. What do you do when your hands are deformed, and the bones disintegrate? You play anyway. Mom played piano with her knuckles (though violin was impossible and the accordion increasingly so). It was a miracle to see someone with hands so severely deformed play better than most. She could easily outplay me (and all my fingers worked!). Her joy is the reason I'm a follower of Jesus. In my nights of questioning whether God was real, she was the light in my darkness. Her hurt became my hope.

There are two extremes to dark places within the Christian community. The first is to complain loudly so that everyone can see how "real" and "transparent" you are. Others marvel that "Christians are just like everyone else." Christians love to hear others complain about how hard times are hard. But complaining doesn't illuminate the dark.

The other extreme is to pretend that nothing is wrong. One staff member was telling me how she got into a car crash and then quickly said, "But praise the Lord!" There's a lot of that kind of thing in Christianity.

We're so worried that others might think we have a lack of faith that we overcompensate. We gloss over depression, famine, sickness, or injustice by declaring God to be Sovereign. It's our way of saying, *Let's not think about it.*

But neither of those extremes is most often displayed in the Bible. The oldest book in the Bible is the story of Job. Through millennia, people have tenaciously held onto a story of suffering and hope because of how universal suffering is to the human experience. Job was in a dark place. He was realistic about it. But that didn't mean he wasn't going to serve God through it. The Bible records that Job did not sin in his response.

So often in Scripture, we read of men and women going through real difficulties. What we find repeatedly is that the best examples come from those who embraced faithfulness through difficult circumstances. Instead of reveling in their complaints, they chose to listen. Instead of asking others to serve them, they served. They learned generosity in scarcity.

One study showed that the wealthier people become, the less generous they become. Hard times can help us understand and practice generosity if we'll choose to learn through them. Poor people can be happy too. Instead of pretending life is good when it's hard, it's okay to acknowledge that you're going through a difficult time. That kind of transparency invites others to carry us through in faith and life. We learn that we are not alone, even if we feel like we are. We learn to trust faith over feeling.

In short, "dark nights" drum into our hearts a devotion to the things of God. When you don't feel like praying, pray; when you don't feel like praising, praise. When you read your Bible and the words stay flat on the page, keep reading. When you can't remember where you put your car keys, let alone memorize a Bible verse, keep trying to learn the verse. The tenacity of faithfulness is what God is teaching you in dark places.

Application

1. Write down a description of your "rock bottom" moment(s).
2. How have you helped others from the bottom of life?
3. Character is revealed. For it to be revealed, it must be forged. Forging requires a fire. It's a process of being hammered in the heat so that the metal can be shaped. In private, without anyone else watching, how is God forging you? How is he teaching you to be awake, aware, and assured?
4. In Matthew 18–20, Jesus teaches the disciples the lesson that the "least will be the greatest." That's a lesson all of us have to learn over and over again. In the "dark night of the soul" how can God be recognized in your life without being blamed? How can grace be practiced when your life feels surrounded by the ungracious?
5. God still loves you. He hasn't left. You might think that the hopes and dreams that you have for your future are no longer possibilities. Write down a prayer giving God control of the destination and the timing of your future.

Where was God?

"I must first have the sense of God's possession of me before I can have the sense of His presence with me." —Watchman Nee

■

"The Lord is near to the brokenhearted and saves the crushed in spirit." —Psalm 34:18

You might be wondering where God is in this story. Where did God go? It seems as if God disappeared while life grew worse for Joseph with each step of attempted obedience. If following God leads us to places and spaces where life is worse than before, what's the point? If God abandons those who follow him, but shows up when things go well, what kind of a God is that?

God was with Joseph throughout the story. The storyteller took great care to introduce small moments of God-sized affirmation and hope. God is always present in our messes; sometimes we just don't notice him.

This chapter requires us to look back and reflect on where God was in Joseph's story. In previous chapters, we've emphasized the circumstances, the influences of others, Joseph's responsibility, and Joseph's attempts to change. In this chapter, we're going to take a high-level look at the story so far, with an eye toward where God was in the midst of it.

I once knew a missionary who called divine moments and interactions "God nods." As we close out the first part of this book, let's touch on some "God nods" in Joseph's story and draw out some insights for yours.

God with Joseph: God Met Joseph in his Dreams

The first place we see God in Joseph's story lies in Joseph's dreams. These dreams came from God himself. Why did Joseph have these dreams when he did? Just think about that for a second. Why *those* dreams at that time to an insecure, alienated teenager?

One reason was that God met Joseph where he was. He met him physically, emotionally, and existentially. Where was Joseph? He was *physically* living in a dysfunctional family where he was isolated and alienated from his brothers. *Emotionally*, he was feeling alone and insecure. The one male figure on his side, his father Jacob, was relationally clueless. Joseph was desperate to connect socially but didn't know how to do it. But God took things one step further and met Joseph where others couldn't. God met him *existentially*. God can reach behind our eyes, into our loneliness.

God was saying, "Joseph, you think you're nothing. But I have created you for something. One day you'll be as significant as you hope." God was encouraging Joseph in his dreams. He was saying, "I have plans for you." When Joseph felt himself to be the smallest and the most unnoticed, God gave Joseph a glimpse of his future. He was letting Joseph know that there was a bigger future ahead. Rather than internalize and embrace God's encouragement and affirmation, Joseph used it as a justification to impress others. God gave Joseph the dreams; he never told Joseph to gather his family around him and share them.

God with Joseph: God Met Joseph in Dothan.

So [Jacob] sent [Joseph] from the Valley of Hebron, and he came to Shechem. And a man found him wandering in the fields. And the man asked him, "What are you seeking?" "I am seeking my brothers," he said. "Tell me, please, where they are pasturing the flock." And the man said, "They have gone away, for I heard them say, 'Let us go to Dothan.'" So Joseph went after his brothers and found them at Dothan. (Gen. 37:14–17)

This man was not named. The text says that the man found Joseph wandering. Wandering implies a sense of being lost. The man said, "Hey, what are you doing walking around with a target as a coat?" Joseph replied, "I'm looking for my brothers." It was more than coincidence that this particular man was the one man who just happened to have overheard his brothers talking with one another. And it was this same man who knew his brothers had decided to go fourteen miles north to Dothan. How did the man know? What were the odds of one man randomly meeting another with information that was specific, timely, and nonthreatening? It's not as if Joseph's brothers were putting up posters all over Shechem: "LOOKING FOR JACOB'S SONS? Call 1-800-FINDUSINDOTHAN to find out more." Of all of the people living in the area of Shechem, this one guy appeared out of nowhere with precisely the right eavesdropping skills to know where Joseph's brothers had gone. The odds against that happening by coincidence are staggering.

For that reason, some scholars believe this was either an angel or a theophany. A theophany is an appearance of Jesus in the Old Testament. Jesus may have shown up in a field to personally direct Joseph!

Even if it wasn't a theophany, it was still a visible instance of God protecting and watching over Joseph. *God entered into Joseph's wandering.* It was an example of God's providential protection and direction as Joseph was wandering around. "Even though I walk through the valley of the shadow of death, I will fear no evil, for you are with me" (Ps. 23:4).

God with Joseph: Together in the Pit

Sometimes, life is the pits. As a prisoner in a Nazi concentration camp in 1944, Corrie ten Boom said, "There is no pit so deep that the love of God is not deeper still." Acts 7:9 reads, "And the patriarchs, jealous of Joseph, sold him into Egypt; but God was with him." God was with Joseph in the pit. Generations of Israelites would remember God's presence there. It's a part of the proclamation of how God is in our darkest places. I love the specificity of the Old Testament here. The text says that Joseph's brothers threw Joseph in a cistern that was not full of water. Well, that's helpful. It would be a short story if it had been full of water. So why did the storyteller point this out? Maybe there were other cisterns, and those cisterns were full of water. The point is that God protected Joseph even in the type of cistern he was thrown into.

Joseph had had a long day, having just walked fourteen miles, when his brothers grabbed him. He hadn't yet eaten. The storyteller highlighted the brothers' cruelty in that detail. His brothers actually ate while Joseph was going hungry in the cistern. And this cistern couldn't be seen from the caravan route, so only certain people would know the location of it. Joseph could have starved to death. But God was with Joseph in the well. God is in our pits.

God with Joseph: Not Just Any Caravan

A caravan arrived, but it was not just any caravan, it was a caravan of Ishmaelites. If the word *Ishmael* in *Ishmaelites* sounds familiar, it's because we talked about Ishmael in chapter one. Ishmael was the illegitimate son Abraham sent away. Ishmael's descendants are the Ishmaelites. These were the same people who picked up Joseph.

Think for a moment of the symmetry and the poetry of what happened. A caravan full of the descendants of an exiled member of Jacob's extended family (Ishmael), came by and picked up the current exile (Joseph) of the family. They were sent by God to take Joseph to the place where God could work on Joseph's character and future.

Currently, my aunt is caring for my uncle, who is moving through the stages of Alzheimer's disease. It's a long and painful journey. But God is in the arduous journey. You might feel helpless in the situation you're in right now. You're in a dark place, and events are sweeping you to destinations unknown. Remember, God is in your caravan. How he is working in your moment might not be visible to you. But he is there.

God with Joseph: In Prison

Joseph found himself in a prison cell for those condemned as enemies of the state. "But the LORD was with Joseph and showed him steadfast love and gave him favor in the sight of the keeper of the prison" (Gen. 39:21). God still loved Joseph! God wasn't absent. In fact, his love was constant for Joseph. God wasn't working to watch Joseph squirm in a prison. There was no glee by God in the cupbearer's forgetfulness. Instead, God was helping Joseph feel his presence and learn to draw his comfort and peace from God alone.

I've been in a few dark places myself. Anyone who has been in a dark place, perhaps the death of someone close to you or the loss of something important, understands how much of a lifeline it is to feel and know God is still with you.

We'd served overseas as church planters for nearly a decade and were in the process of transitioning back to the United States. For a variety of reasons, I was in transition from an incredible mission organization. We were in an odd position where I could not yet obtain other full-time employment. Still, because of our circumstances, I was also earning 80 percent of my previous income. And because we were transitioning, expenses went up. We kept praying and following Jesus through it all (my wife was especially wonderful during this time).

For two months, we didn't have enough money to purchase groceries. My wife, still positive and encouraging, suggested we give blood to make ends meet. The first time we went was humiliating for me. I was well-educated with a great resume but was giving blood for groceries. Still, we continued to remain positive and pray.

The next month, things turned worse. As I was trying to donate blood, I had an adverse physical reaction. I was no longer allowed to donate. Humiliated twice over, I returned to my car and wept as my wife finished the process of giving her blood. Afterward, we drove to the grocery store, and I felt as low as I've ever felt.

As bad as things were, though, we knew we were making the right decisions. We didn't complain about our predicament, though we also didn't like it. God was with us. Within the next three months, we would not only have enough money to purchase groceries but were able to set money aside in savings. God was with us, and we knew it. During that time, this was sometimes the only consolation I had as husband and provider. Following God in the darkness is one way of learning how to follow him in the light.

God was with Joseph not only by his presence but also by actively showing Joseph his steadfast love. When we reap the consequences of godly choices, we also receive a God who is with us through those choices. God was pouring out his love for Joseph. Joseph's life may not have been pleasant, but it was better than if there had been no God with him. You can live in the dark without God or with God. The former will lead you to place your hope in coincidences or competencies to get you out. The latter will lead you to trust in a God who is more powerful than coincidences or competencies.

The dark places may be dark, but it's often *to* dark places that light must travel. We just think we'll go there volitionally. But sometimes, we don't. That doesn't mean God isn't leading. God wants to shape us in the context of dark places to bring beauty there too. Joseph may have been the man God used to bring humanity to the insanity of a prison. Joseph became the encouragement others needed. Joseph learned empathy in prison. He learned how to find his significance in simply serving the Lord rather than in the affirmation of others. In prison, Joseph was affirmed both in his competencies and in his character, but he no longer needed others to affirm him in order to know his worth.

Lessons from God's Presence in our Messes

1. The journey is a part of the destination.

God allowed Joseph to languish in jail because of—not in spite of—his love for Joseph. Joseph had natural hopes and expectations. It's okay to have hopes and expectations. But remember that God has the ability and timing. That's where your hope resides.

God was shifting Joseph's character and guiding him to progress in spiritual maturity. The Joseph who emerged from prison was a different man from the one who went into it. Joseph was on a journey of character change. Little by little, God was forging his own character traits in Joseph's attitudes and actions.

Throughout the Bible, we often see that character is revealed in testing and forged in faithfulness. We sometimes wish Joseph's character change, forged by fire to reflect God's character, involved just one test or trial. But sometimes, it takes many tests and trials to create in us the heart that God wants.

So often, we try to predict how we'll be significant to God. We have dreams for ourselves and believe we know the pathway to the realization of those dreams. But God sees further.

2. Life can be unfair, but you don't have to be unfair too.

Joseph did not appear bitter through his trial. He hatched no revenge plan on Potiphar's wife. There was no passive-aggressive response from Joseph to God. He didn't attempt to make Potiphar's wife feel guilty or make her pay for her lies. Joseph understood that *sinful people behave sinfully*. That doesn't excuse their sinfulness, but it does help inform our own response by reminding us that they are consistent in their behavior.

The New Testament records that a man named Stephen was stoned to death. As he was being stoned, he said, "Lord, do not hold this sin against them" (Acts 7:60). This is reminiscent of Jesus's request on the cross, "Father, forgive them, for they know not what they do" (Lk. 23:34). You can spend your life being angry at people who behave according to their nature, or you can recognize their anger is born from a place of fragmentation, hurt, and ignorance. Anger breeds more anger, resentment, and resignation. By choosing to see the context, you're giving permission to your anger to give way to understanding. You'll know the truth and it will set you free (John 8:32).

Difficulties will tempt us to resent the people or circumstances life throws our way. God isn't teaching us to put ourselves on display as the victims of this cruel life. Too often, Christians are treated poorly and then go on a social media rant to talk about how unfairly they were treated by others. Righteous indignation can sometimes stink up social media. Joseph did the right thing and paid a terrible cost. Yet, he did not allow another's cruelty to determine his emotional state. Joseph didn't wallow in misery. Instead, he kept his eyes on God. No, he was not thrilled to be in prison. This is not a lesson about pleasure in pain. It's a lesson on a godly response to unfair accusations and life circumstances.

The apostle Paul wrote, "For the desires of the flesh are against the Spirit, and the desires of the Spirit are against the flesh, for these are opposed to each other, to keep you from doing the things you want to do" (Gal. 5:17). If we pursue what we want, we may be acting in opposition to the life God wants for us. In other words, elite French models can be miserable, too. Both poor and wealthy people get depressed and commit suicide.

One of our most popular hymns is "Amazing Grace," a hymn penned by a former ship's captain who had transported slaves as cargo. On his own, the captain was pursuing wealth for the sake of wealth. His contribution to human trafficking was monumental. And then the captain met Jesus, and everything changed. It was this man, through tears of gratitude and grace, that God would use to pen these lyrics: "*Amazing grace, how sweet the sound, that saved a wretch like me.*" History has forgotten the slave ship captain, but it has not forgotten the man who wrote "Amazing Grace." Which person will you be?

3. Remember, it's not over yet.

Tony Campolo wrote a famous sermon and book with the title *It's Friday, but Sunday's Coming!* He was referring to the hopelessness on the Friday night that Jesus was crucified, and the hope of Sunday morning. You might think you're too old, too far gone, or too much in a hole. But God has radically turned around the lives of all kinds of people in all kinds of situations. You might say, "That's impossible!" The disciples once asked Jesus about where hope was for the unlikely. "But Jesus looked at them and said, 'With man this is impossible, but with God all things are possible'" (Matt. 19:26).

My hope is that you're moving away from the status quo that leads to so much helplessness. But you may still be in Part One of your journey. Be careful not to lose perspective and think this is the whole of your life. Don't believe the lie that you're a "good-for-nothing" person. "And we know that for those who love God all things work together for good, for those who are called according to his purpose" (Rom. 8:28). God doesn't create worthless people. You were created with purpose, hope, and worth. The caveat in Romans 8:28 is that it's for "those who love God." Love God in the dark. The light is coming.

APPLICATION

Do you believe that God is with you right now?
1. Look back and write down some ways you can see how God was with you in your past messes.
2. Take a moment to thank him for being with you. He is in your hopes, journeys, and pits of despair.

PART TWO

HIS
MASTERPIECE

7

My Life is Turning Around!

"Success always demands a greater effort." —*Winston Churchill*

■

"And Pharaoh said to Joseph, 'I have had a dream, and there is no one who can interpret it. I have heard it said of you that when you hear a dream you can interpret it.'" —*Genesis 41:15*

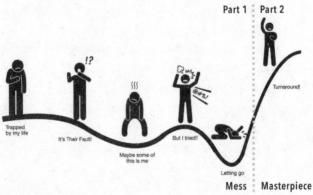

M anaging a blessing is as challenging as managing a curse. P Diddy once sang, "Mo' money, mo' problems." It's a good thing God took Joseph to the deepest valley, because Joseph would need all the traits he learned there in the places of prominence and influence that lay before him. While he was learning to let go, God was leading him to a turnaround.

Joseph went through the wringer, so that God could do in him what was required. Joseph developed empathy and a heart for others. He understood how to recognize a divine moment. He learned how to step into that moment with discernment and with a humble spirit that rooted its confidence in God.

Country singer Tim McGraw says he lives by "one key value." A report by the *Today Show* on NBC recounts an Instagram story posted by the star:

That value is, be ready. Be primed for opportunity when it shows up, because it will come once, it will move on quick, and if you're not ready to make the shot, your whole destiny can change in a heartbeat. Miss that moment, and you'll live the rest of your life wondering just how much of your potential never played out.

McGraw cites many examples where his ability to recognize and seize a moment has significantly shaped his life. But one small moment might surprise you. His daughter was watching a movie in which he starred and commented she thought he looked "big on screen." While many would have let that moment pass, Tim McGraw viewed it as an opportunity to make significant changes in his health. He dropped forty pounds, opened a gym, and is now renowned for his commitment to fitness. So many people allow small moments to pass them by. Moments come our way all the time. How many of them do we miss?

Other moments aren't so small. Dr. Erwin Lutzer tells of the moment that led up to the invitation to him to become the senior pastor of the historic Moody Church in downtown Chicago. After resigning from his previous church, he and his wife were seeking a church to visit on the first Sunday of April. Ten minutes before the service began, he ran into Warren Wiersbe, who was the current pastor. Wiersbe told Lutzer he was sick and asked him if he would preach for him that morning. Lutzer recognized the moment, accepted, and preached. He seized the divine moment God provided. Where most would have said, "It's too late," Dr. Lutzer recognized the timeliness of God. Soon after, Dr. Lutzer was asked to serve as the lead pastor of Moody Church.

Knowing Your Moment in Time

In the Bible, there are two big ideas for time. The first is *chronos*. It's from this word that we get the idea of chronology. Chronos is a moment in time. Your birthday is in the *chronos* of time. The second is *kairos*. Kairos is the idea of being on time. Certain moments require a sense of timing. Kairos is that sense of timing. *Chronos* tells you that you'll graduate on a specific day. *Kairos* tells you the timeliness of your career choices.

Sometimes, the two ideas exist simultaneously. For example, Easter Sunday is a moment of *chronos*, but it can also be a powerful moment of *kairos*. As a pastor, I have to prepare accordingly. But while they can exist at the same time, most divine moments have less to do with *chronos* than *kairos*. Moments are often timely but unexpected. And God is in control of the timing.

Erwin McManus was pastoring a small church in a poor urban Texas community and working as a street evangelist. One day a youth conference was held in his town, and he volunteered to work in the parking lot. A leader walked up to him and said by God's prompting, he felt Erwin was to speak at that conference. Quickly changing from his street clothes, Erwin borrowed clothes that didn't fit him. But Erwin recognized this was his *kairos* moment. Sure enough, preaching at that youth conference launched Erwin onto the national stage as a speaker. Today, he talks to packed venues all over the world.

What's important is that in all three of these stories—McGraw, Lutzer, McManus—the context of their small and big moments was a context of faithfulness. McGraw already had the value of "be ready" before his daughter spoke. Lutzer was already faithfully preaching and then pursuing his education. McManus was already regularly preaching and evangelizing on the streets of his Texas town. Character is forged in faithfulness. Character is *revealed* in testing. Sometimes we like what that revelation says about us, and sometimes we don't. But we're all asked to step into the *kairos* moments that await us in the context of faithfulness.

Joseph's Divine Moment

Genesis chapter 41 begins with this statement, "After two whole years, Pharaoh dreamed that he was standing by the Nile." In the last chapter, I talked about the difficulty and value of those two years for Joseph. But it would be narrow to think God was confined to working just in Joseph's life during that timeframe. God was at work in others to set up his *kairos*.

God was at work in Pharaoh. God gave Pharaoh a dream at exactly the right time. It was a time where the cupbearer was back and had built up enough credibility to be heard. It was a time where Pharaoh was so desperate and "troubled" to have his dream interpreted that he launched an urgent search for wisdom. He was desperate for insight beyond himself.

God longs to witness to others through his followers. I've had avowed atheists ask me to pray for them. God is providing that individual their own divine moment to place their faith and life in a God who is real. When someone is desperate for answers, they don't play games. They go where the power is. The Egyptian sun-god, Ra, wasn't doing anything for Pharaoh. How would Pharaoh know of Yahweh, who was (and is) greater? God put someone in his proximity who would be pivotal to Pharaoh's success as a ruler.

God was also at work in cultural acclimation. God needed a son of Jacob, and an outsider who was not from Egypt, to know enough about Egyptian culture, language, and customs, that he could be heard and seen appropriately within Egypt. Moreover, God wanted to position someone who could speak with royalty. Not even Egyptian peasants or the working class could do that! How, then, can an outsider—someone without the language, knowledge of the upper class, position in the royal court, or understanding of the complex conversations and political dynamics at work—become an insider? First, God placed Joseph under the care of Potiphar, the captain of the royal guards, who was personally familiar with Pharaoh. Second, God put Joseph in a jail designed for the king's prisoners. There Joseph had personal interaction with those who'd gone against Pharaoh and failed. Third, Joseph helped two men who interacted with Pharaoh regularly. They knew his personality and the rules of court.

There's an old saying that any one person is only separated by another socially anywhere on the planet by six degrees. Physicist and network theorist Albert-László Barabási has demonstrated that this number is likely less. For Joseph, the distance from an obscure Israelite to the most powerful man in Egypt narrowed from six to two degrees of separation. One invitation to speak to Pharaoh is all it would take for Joseph's *kairos* moment to appear.

Remember that in Joseph, unshaken confidence in God was forged. The heat of the forge took the form of suffering and endurance. But both produced peace amid storms. Joseph would not be overwhelmed by someone as prominent as Pharaoh.

Because of his time in prison, Joseph had experience interpreting the dreams of others. Joseph knew how to deliver the good *and* bad news of dream interpretations. He did not flinch when he let the baker know that the baker would die. And this was after getting to know the baker, empathizing and listening to him. Joseph learned to speak confidently but with humility. Joseph had learned to tell the truth, good and bad.

Also, imagine how useful that sense of calm and peace would be when a seven-year famine would later hit Egypt. Joseph could not have foreseen what was coming, but God was at work, providing opportunities for Joseph to learn. Joseph had a lot to absorb, including language, culture, customs, people, nuance, courage, integrity, devotion, and empathy. Over and over, God would provide *chronos* and *kairos* moments for Joseph. Joseph would learn faithfulness. Remember, *character is forged in faithfulness.*

We all want *chronos*. We want things today and in our timeline. But God uses *chronos* as a means of setting up his *kairos*. It's the *chronos* that makes us ready. The dates and hours will arrive. It's the *kairos* that determines our readiness.

Joseph: Between Two Worlds

All Christians live between two worlds.

And behold, there came up out of the Nile seven cows, attractive and plump, and they fed in the reed grass. And behold, seven other cows, ugly and thin, came up out of the Nile after them, and stood by the other cows on the bank of the Nile. And the ugly, thin cows ate up the seven attractive, plump cows. And Pharaoh awoke. And he fell asleep and dreamed a second time. And behold, seven ears of grain, plump and good, were growing on one stalk. And behold, after them sprouted seven ears, thin and blighted by the east wind. And the thin ears swallowed up the seven plump, full ears. And

Pharaoh awoke, and behold, it was a dream. So in the morning his spirit was troubled, and he sent and called for all the magicians of Egypt and all its wise men. Pharaoh told them his dreams, but there was none who could interpret them to Pharaoh.

Then the chief cupbearer said to Pharaoh, "I remember my offenses today. When Pharaoh was angry with his servants and put me and the chief baker in custody in the house of the captain of the guard, we dreamed on the same night, he and I, each having a dream with its own interpretation. A young Hebrew was there with us, a servant of the captain of the guard. When we told him, he interpreted our dreams to us, giving an interpretation to each man according to his dream. And as he interpreted to us, so it came about. I was restored to my office, and the baker was hanged."

Then Pharaoh sent and called Joseph, and they quickly brought him out of the pit. And when he had shaved himself and changed his clothes, he came in before Pharaoh. And Pharaoh said to Joseph, "I have had a dream, and there is no one who can interpret it. I have heard it said of you that when you hear a dream you can interpret it." Joseph answered Pharaoh, "It is not in me; God will give Pharaoh a favorable answer." (Gen. 41:2–16)

Notice that before speaking to Pharaoh, Joseph dressed and shaved to look Egyptian. He was made presentable to Pharaoh in the Egyptian way. "Then Pharaoh sent and called Joseph, and they quickly brought him out of the pit. And when he had shaved himself and changed his clothes, he came in before Pharaoh." Sometimes Christians believe this to be some sort of compromise. Many Christians today would snort and say, "Joseph had no courage! He kowtowed to the world!" But so often, we confuse the outward with the inward. God is concerned that our values are not the world's values. He wants to be Lord over our hearts. The style of dress one wears is secondary to the character of the person wearing it. Joseph was no longer wearing Hebrew garb, dressed as a distinctive outsider. In fact, from this point onward, for the rest of Joseph's life, he would talk and dress like an Egyptian.

It's helpful to acknowledge that the cupbearer also seized his *kairos* moment. Just as none of Pharaoh's "wise men" could interpret the dream, the cupbearer said, "I remember my offenses today." He then factually and with no embellishments, recounted what had happened earlier. He allowed Pharaoh to do with the information whatever Pharaoh wanted. The cupbearer knew that this was an opportune moment where he could speak of Joseph to Pharaoh. Perhaps he also had a sense of regret that he hadn't (or couldn't have) spoken of Joseph to Pharaoh appropriately earlier. The cupbearer saw the right moment, a moment that preserved his own life and position while also potentially helping Pharaoh. He told the story of a Hebrew man in prison who had helped him personally by interpreting his divine dream.

When Joseph was brought before Pharaoh, he 1) did not know Pharaoh's dream, and 2) did not know if he could interpret it. Notice Joseph's humility. "And Pharaoh said to Joseph, 'I have had a dream, and there is no one who can interpret it. I have heard it said of you that when you hear a dream you can interpret it.' Joseph answered Pharaoh, 'It is not in me; God will give Pharaoh a favorable answer'" (Gen. 41:15–16). This is a very different Joseph! He's no longer saying, "I'm the guy! See how special I am." Instead, he knew that this moment was utterly dependent on God. Putting Joseph's situation into perspective, Joseph did not know if God *would* provide an interpretation. But Joseph had learned his worth was based on God alone—answer or no answer.

Pharaoh gave two dreams with similar components. Seven fat cows and seven good stalks. Thin cows ate fat cows. Cows seem harmless until they're bloodthirsty. There's a horror movie with the terrifying premise of sheep who become bloodthirsty killers. It was created and filmed in New Zealand, which is a country full of sheep. Same idea. Thin cows eating fat cows in vivid detail would have been disturbing. Then thin stalks ate fat stalks. The subsequent dream of stalks had to have been more confusing, which is why Pharaoh didn't put two and two together. For an agrarian society, these vivid dreams are disturbing. Small wonder Pharaoh was desperate for an answer.

Joseph began with the obvious and then moved to interpretation. "The dreams of Pharaoh are one; God has revealed to Pharaoh what he is about to do" (v. 25). Joseph must have felt calm and confident at this point. One would also imagine that he must have also been a little relieved. In that *kairos* moment God provided Joseph an interpretation of Pharaoh's dreams. God was right on time. That allowed Joseph to speak calmly and insightfully.

> Then Joseph said to Pharaoh, "The dreams of Pharaoh are one; God has revealed to Pharaoh what he is about to do. . . . There will come seven years of great plenty throughout all the land of Egypt, but after them there will arise seven years of famine, and all the plenty will be forgotten in the land of Egypt. The famine will consume the land, and the plenty will be unknown in the land by reason of the famine that will follow, for it will be very severe. And the doubling of Pharaoh's dream means that the thing is fixed by God, and God will shortly bring it about. (Gen. 41:25–32)

To speak insightfully, Joseph had to trust God despite the relational complexity of the moment. There was an unhealthy social dynamic into which Joseph had walked. The text tells us that Pharaoh called all of the "magicians of Egypt and all its wise men." Where were they when Joseph stood before Pharaoh? Many were likely in the room! If you've ever walked into an awkward moment, that's the kind of moment into which Joseph walked. This would be like walking in on a married couple fighting, or a staff conflict. That would be like social dynamite with a fuse ready to be lit. It was into those dynamics, between those who would pretend to be magical and those who would seek out good judgment, that Joseph spoke. He went unaware. Joseph stood dressed as an Egyptian, functioning as another wise man for Pharaoh. He didn't realize he was competing with the other wise men and magicians. A question mark loomed in the room: who is this man? What could he possibly have to say or do that is wiser than the wise men, or more fantastic than the magicians? In those moments, we have to trust God.

God was the only one, except perhaps for the cupbearer, who believed in Joseph.

When I was in high school, I found myself as the only Christ-follower in my sociology class. My teacher was an ardent agnostic who loved nothing more than to pit the class against itself. He believed robust arguments led to better learning. He would often divide the classroom up for "hot topics." Everyone "in favor" on one side of the room and everyone "against" on the other side. On more than one occasion, I would find myself alone on one side of the room. But this had two effects on me. First, it caused me to think through why I stood on that side. Second, it caused me to have even greater confidence in God's perspective.

When my oldest son was in school in Austria, he wasn't just the only Christ-follower in his class. He was the only one in his school. He was in the minority. But what were his alternatives? He could pretend to be in the majority but secretly stand for God. But they would sniff out his allegiances pretty quickly. He could behave like everyone else did and engage in the social dysfunctions of teenage angst, in a desperate attempt to blend in. Or he could follow the biblical patterns of relationships (don't gossip, tell the truth, be kind, be friendly, etc.). In the former, he might get caught up in the same types of relational patterns they were all in. By the latter, he could forge a new path that would ultimately help him navigate life. When we are faced with relational complexity, the choice is straightforward: stay close to God. Unfortunately, so many of us make the opposite choice. When the dynamics get complicated, we play along with the relational games others want to create. We participate in meetings before meetings. We pit people against each other. We learn to survive by playing according to the rules in the room. The only problem is that those rules are flawed.

How do we know Joseph stayed close to God? After Joseph interpreted Pharaoh's dreams, Pharaoh said, "Can we find a man like this, in whom is the Spirit of God?" Notice that power is attributed to God, even as Joseph is associated with being God's man. Then Pharaoh said to Joseph, "Since God has shown you all this, there is none so discerning and wise as you are." How else can we speak insightfully? Joseph listened carefully and actively to Pharaoh's dreams. He made sure he could repeat the details. Joseph sought to understand what God was saying and doing in the life of someone else.

Too often, we dismiss that which we can't understand. We belittle legitimate opportunities for conversations. We laugh at silly dreams. Sometimes, we make a recommendation before really listening to what the other person is saying. We're so busy thinking about our solutions, and we miss their descriptions regarding their interactions with God. We nod and recommend some warm milk and melatonin before the person goes to sleep next time. We're not actively listening and considering that God is speaking uniquely to them. If we did, our patent answers might not work. So, we reframe their experiences into something we can inform. But Joseph took seriously that the dreams were from Yahweh and that they held meaning for the dreamer. In this case, he saw they held meaning for Egypt and the surrounding nations as well.

Joseph saw God's divine hand at work in their dreams. He understood that what was coming was an opportunity for faithfulness in preparation. God warned Pharaoh for a reason. And so, he not only rightly interpreted the dreams but also provided a recommendation for moving forward. This recommendation was practical and helpful. In verse thirty-two, he explained the reason there were two dreams. The second emphasized the certainty of the first. The *chronos* were "fixed by God." Knowing the *chronos* allowed Joseph to make a *kairos* recommendation. In verses 34–36, he presented a proposal for what to do about it. He didn't just say, "Here's what God is saying to you. Good luck with that!" Instead, he set forward a proposal, a recommendation for action, that would require no small amount of intentionality and leadership on the part of Pharaoh. Joseph told Pharaoh, the highest person with the most amount of power in all of Egypt, what and how he should lead over the next fourteen years. It was strategic and specific. Let's look at the *details*.

Let Pharaoh proceed to appoint overseers over the land and take one-fifth of the produce of the land of Egypt during the seven plentiful years. And let them gather all the food of these good

years that are coming and store up grain under the authority of
Pharaoh for food in the cities, and let them keep it. That food shall
be a reserve for the land against the seven years of famine that
are to occur in the land of Egypt, so that the land may not perish
through the famine." (Gen. 41:34–36)

Here again are the bullet points of Joseph's proposal:

- Select a wise and discerning man and set him over the land of
  Egypt.
- Appoint overseers over the land.
- Take one-fifth of the harvest during the plentiful years and store
  up the grain.
- The food is a reserve, so have a system in place to distribute it back
  when the famine hits.

Remember, this is all in the context of answering a dream. Joseph
did not have to give a recommendation. He could have done what was
in his own best interest, which in this case would be to interpret the
dream, leaving out key details. That way, Joseph could make himself
indispensable in the coming years, doling out a new aspect as needed. Or,
if he won his freedom by interpreting the dream, he could have made his
way back to his father and brothers and prepared them and that country
for the years ahead. Instead, Joseph made a recommendation designed to
help and bless his captors.

Consider these words from a letter in Jeremiah 29 by God to his
people in exile, held captive in a foreign country. Instead of instructing
them in the ways of guerilla warfare, God told his people to be a blessing:

Thus says the LORD of hosts, the God of Israel, to all the exiles whom
I have sent into exile from Jerusalem to Babylon: Build houses and
live in them; plant gardens and eat their produce. Take wives and
have sons and daughters; take wives for your sons, and give your
daughters in marriage, that they may bear sons and daughters;

multiply there, and do not decrease. But seek the welfare of the city where I have sent you into exile, and pray to the LORD on its behalf, for in its welfare you will find your welfare. . . . When seventy years are completed for Babylon, I will visit you, and I will fulfill to you my promise and bring you back to this place. For I know the plans I have for you, declares the LORD, plans for welfare and not for evil, to give you a future and a hope. Then you will call upon me and come and pray to me, and I will hear you. You will seek me and find me, when you seek me with all your heart. (Jer. 29:4–13)

In the welfare of Egypt, Joseph would find his well-being. Why? Because God alone knew the plans he had for Joseph, and Joseph trusted in God's plans for him. So, Joseph did what was right, not what was most convenient.

People around us are desperate for insight. They long for others to see in them what they cannot see for themselves. They hope to be taken seriously in their inner turmoil and spiritual dialogue. And they would love someone to make a smart, specific recommendation. Not a rote proposal. Not the same prescription many give: "Say this prayer and call me in the morning." Instead, they're looking for truths that meet them where they are and call them to something greater. In short, they're looking for a blessing.

Joseph provided a recommendation to Pharaoh that called Pharaoh to exceptional leadership. Pharaoh responded not by personally providing that leadership, but instead by identifying the leader in front of him. He knew that Joseph was wise, courageous, insightful, and filled with integrity. He didn't need his magicians or wise men in the years ahead because they all had competing agendas. Joseph aimed to please God and bless Egypt. So, Pharaoh put Joseph in charge of . . . everything.

This is the moment of victory and redemption for which we've been waiting. Read it and smile, "You shall be over my house, and all my people shall order themselves as you command. Only as regards the throne will I be greater than you. . . . See, I have set you over all the land of Egypt" (Gen. 41:40–41). If this were a *Star Wars* film, this would be the moment Luke, Hans Solo, and Chewbacca walk forward to receive medals. Roll credits. Joseph was thirty years old when this moment of victory happened.

Joseph would follow through on his proposal for Pharaoh, and he was diligent in setting up this massive system of gathering and storing grain. Egypt had bread during a time when no one had grain. When things grew worse in Egypt, Pharaoh's only instructions were, "Go to Joseph. What he says to you, do" (Gen. 41:55). Ultimately, not only did the Egyptians come to Joseph. So too did "all the earth" (v. 57). God brought the nations to the boy who was once sold into slavery. The same boy who ran from temptation showed integrity with the grain. The empathy Joseph learned in prison became the empathy he used in dealing wisely with hungry, desperate people. Pharaoh became very wealthy. Egypt rose to become a powerful nation because of the immense leverage they had in providing food for hungry immigrants. All because someone spoke with authority to bring a plan to fruition.

In Mark 1:17, Jesus called his disciples to be "fishers of men." The first place he led them was to a worship service in Capernaum. It was there they learned what it meant to "speak with authority." The text repeats that phrase twice. We are to speak confidently and humbly as followers of Jesus. Joseph learned how to speak with authority.

In Luke 10, Jesus sent out seventy-two disciples. He gave them specific instructions, including their prime focus, which was to seek out a person of peace in the village and bless them and their household. This seemed like an odd instruction until we look back into the Old Testament to understand that it is consistent with God. Bless the place or the people where God puts you, whether in a new village, a church, in exile, prison, or before a Pharaoh. Choose to be a blessing.

Peter and John stood before the Sanhedrin. They were on trial in a relationally complex and tense dynamic. What did they do to be on trial? They blessed a man by healing him. In speaking to the Sanhedrin, they spoke of how Jesus had interacted with them. They spoke to the spiritual bind the Sanhedrin was in. And they gave specific recommendations for finding hope in that bind.

"This Jesus is the stone that was rejected by you, the builders, which has become the cornerstone. And there is salvation in no one else, for there is no other name under heaven given among men by which we must be saved." Now when they saw the boldness of Peter and John and perceived that they were uneducated, common men, they were astonished. And they recognized that they had been with Jesus. But seeing the man who was healed standing beside them, they had nothing to say in opposition. (Acts 4:11–14).

They spoke humbly, confidently, and insightfully. Sound familiar?

In life, there are pharaohs everywhere. Every day, ordinary people are called by God to stand before them. Stepping into a divine moment with humble confidence in God, we listen and speak to the conversation God is having with them, and with specific insight into what could help. Yes, the *chronos* has changed. But the *kairos* is what counts.

Lessons from the Turnaround

1. Don't confuse sharing clothes with sharing values.

Do not love the world or the things in the world. If anyone loves the world, the love of the Father is not in him. For all that is in the world—the desires of the flesh and the desires of the eyes and pride of life—is not from the Father but is from the world. And the world is passing away along with its desires, but whoever does the will of God abides forever. (1 John 2:15–17)

Scripture is clear that change begins in the heart. We simply shouldn't value the same things the world does. In the passage from 1 John above, it's the desires of the flesh (wanting what the world wants), and the wants of the eyes (wanting what I want), and pride of life (wanting status).

But what *should* we wear? It depends on your mission field. What are the people wearing that God is calling you to reach? In Joseph's case,

God made sure Joseph looked and walked Egyptian, though his heart and identity were Hebrew.

Too often, we confuse clothes, music, movies, or culture with values. But they aren't necessarily connected. Joseph dressed as an Egyptian, but his heart and life belonged to God.

Maybe the reason so many Christians rail against culture is that it's easier to fix which movies you allow yourself to see than change your heart. Instead of dealing with gossip, anger, jealousy, or pettiness, we focus on dress, school, or job status. Christians who grew up in church can get away with being spiteful because they know which signals to send. But God looks deeper.

Notice, however, that though Joseph's heart does not belong to the Egyptians, God has given Joseph a place to belong. Joseph will always associate with Egyptians. He will pour his life into leading and blessing them. Where Joseph once felt lonely, he was lonely no more.

When you find inner health, God begins to adjust your circumstances. He not only provides an avenue for you to grow in your competencies, but he also grafts you into his church. Where you may have once been lonely or isolated, you now have a family. Sometimes, this will feel strange. People will sing songs and speak in terms that are unique to their Christian subculture. But you will have found a new community of belonging.

2. When the moment arrives, don't shrink back.

There's an old saying: The devil you know is better than the devil you don't. But we lose many opportunities for God's best when we think that way. Don't miss your moment.

Some moments may be small. Someone may ask you to say a prayer at the evening meal. Step up and pray. Someone may ask you to serve in a church. Step up and serve. The moment is there by design. Have the courage to recognize that God has it there for a reason.

I have a fear of heights. If I'm not careful, my fear will dictate my actions. I'll miss out on incredible vistas or opportunities. That doesn't make my fear go away. But when I choose courage, I'm reminding myself that fear doesn't rule me. That's why I went skydiving with my sons. I refused to trade a father-sons experience for fear.

Every day, we have to have the courage to make choices away from the fears that are always present. You might be shy. Your biggest fear is that you'll have to "go public." But when the moment arrives, don't let fear win. Each choice for courage is a reminder that you are capable of more than you may think.

Ask an alcoholic if he or she is sober, and they'll tell you that each day is a choice for sobriety. Each day is a moment to see the benefits of the new you, a moment to step into faith. You're no longer the person you once were. This is the moment to know that God owns your heart, and that "The old has passed away; behold, the new has come" (2 Cor. 5:17). "Behold, I am doing a new thing; now it springs forth, do you not perceive it?" (Isa. 43:19)

Seize your divine moment. If you're an employee, don't just do what's asked. Seize the day and suggest a new initiative or idea. Add value to your employer beyond the tasks for which you are being paid. If you're a father, don't merely provide. Seize the day by finding creative ways to instruct, love, or share yourself. If you're a church member, don't just attend. Ask yourself how you can help the church fulfill its vision and mission. Seize the day. You never know what will happen. You may even find yourself in charge of a nation.

3. Listen carefully to understand and bless.

The most beneficial skill you can master is the skill of listening. Listening means hearing what is said and what isn't. Some people listen factually. That is appropriate at times. But try to listen to the tone, context, and subtext.

You are not the first person to be in conversation with others. God arrived before you did. Before Joseph had a dream to interpret, God spoke to Pharaoh in a dream. God speaks through circumstances and other people. God speaks mostly through his Word. Listen to what he is saying and seek to understand what you're hearing.

The Christian music group Out of the Grey once sang, "He is not silent. He is not whispering. We are not quiet. We are not listening." They're right. What is God saying to the people around you? What's his tone? What openings is he providing you to reiterate or participate in the God-conversations happening around you every day?

When we bless, we're working for the well-being of where we live, work, and play. Sometimes divine work is practical work. It's starting a business, encouraging excellent city infrastructure, or paying attention to public policies. Where are the points of need? What dreams are confusing to the community that surrounds you? What's the best future for the world around you? Start working toward that.

APPLICATION

1. Describe which two worlds has God positioned you for uniquely.
2. How do you stand out from others in your relationship network? What about your character would make others say, "Can we find a [person] like this, in whom is the Spirit of God?"
3. Become a student of divine conversations happening around you. For the next 3–5 days, take time to observe and notice the ways that God is speaking to others in your relationship networks.
4. Your today connects to your tomorrow. What are you cultivating today that God can use in your tomorrow? Which disciplines, attitudes, skills, or actions are you learning in the short term so that God can use them in the long term?
5. You cannot predict your tomorrow. Your safety is not guaranteed. Neither are your financial, occupational, or familial securities. As you look at your current situation, which small moments of opportunity is God presenting you that might position you for an unexpected future?

Renegotiating Relationships

"Happiness is having a large, loving, caring, close-knit family in another city." —George Burns

■

"And Joseph recognized his brothers, but they did not recognize him."
—Genesis 42:8

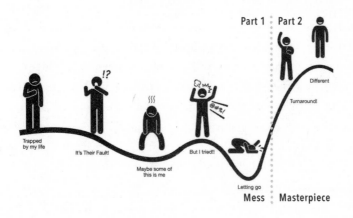

I once attended a leadership retreat in a small rural village in northwest China when, during a session break, I decided to call my wife. As we spoke, I had the feeling eyes were peering at me. Turning around slowly, I told my wife, "You're not going to believe this, but a wild ostrich is staring at me." Then the ostrich started to run at me.

I only know two things about ostriches: 1) they're big, and 2) they're mean. I threw myself over a low Chinese garden wall as the ostrich charged. Then it slowed down, looked around, and kept walking. It made a right-hand turn at the end of the street, and I never saw it again. I looked. What's a rogue ostrich doing in a remote Chinese village?! Sometimes, life throws you an ostrich out of nowhere.

One of our church members was at the top of his profession. Everything seemed perfect. Then one day, his mind suddenly dredged up long-forgotten memories. Buried memories. Memories of abuse and hurt. His hand started shaking and didn't stop. He found himself close to a breakdown. With sustained prayer and the fellowship of our church wrapped around him, he began to navigate his way through a long-forgotten past. Out of nowhere, his personal history threw his life off kilter—like a rogue ostrich.

Ever notice that as soon as you've built a new life, and you have some wind in your sails, a rogue wave comes and tries to capsize your momentum? This is so common that movie plots are built around this reality. The protagonist is doing well, and this leaves the watcher suspicious. We know something or someone is going to try and knock them over. How different is he or she? Will they be able to withstand the coming storm, or will it blow them off course? You may have found a new life, a new approach, and you know that you're a different person from who you were before. But all of this relies on momentum. As long as your past hurts or issues aren't triggered, you're fine. But God wants to teach you how to deal with your past, not ignore it. Life may be unpredictable, but that doesn't mean it's without purpose.

The band Genesis wrote a song called "No Son of Mine." It's the story of a man trying to renegotiate his past. In the next couple of chapters, we're going to examine how Joseph renegotiated his, and then we'll learn from his example. You are not who you once were. Your inner turmoil is no longer dictating your misery. But facing up to your history, especially when it's uninvited, is a whole other challenge.

For context, it's taken five chapters for Joseph to go from being held captive in a pit in Dothan to being second in command in Egypt. The Bible dedicates the next five and a half chapters of Joseph's story to his reconciliation with his family. The amount of space dedicated to family reconciliation tells us a couple of things. First, family reconciliation is complicated. It can be difficult, frustrating, and emotionally charged. Second, time *doesn't* heal all wounds. Sometimes, it just masks them.

Joseph's Perfect Life Interrupted

Joseph was around forty years old when a rogue ostrich charged his perfect life. His family's past reached out to his present. Until this point in his story, none of his brothers had tried to find him. His father thought he was dead. Joseph had spent more than half of his life in Egypt and had a family and a life of his own.

We can only speculate why Joseph, the second most powerful man in that part of the world at that time, did not reach back to a family he missed and loved. One Egyptologist asserts that a palace found in Egypt was once occupied by a non-Egyptian where the number twelve figures prominently. That scholar argues that "twelve" stands for the twelve tribes of Israel and that the palace was Joseph's. It's difficult to know if that is true, but Joseph probably thought about his family through the years. He either consciously or subconsciously referred to his past.

When we first moved to Germany, I was more Californian than when we'd lived in California. Suddenly, my vocabulary included the word "dude" more frequently! We tend to try and hold onto that which makes us unique. We all have ways of marking our histories. Joseph continued to worship Yahweh, although Egyptian gods surrounded him. It must have been isolating to worship Yahweh alone. And Joseph knew the promise given to his great-grandfather Abraham, so the thought of family was meaningful.

Or maybe Joseph was done with that chapter of his life. Perhaps he wanted to let sleeping dogs lie and thought it best to move on. What was past was gone. His family never came looking for him, and he might have questioned, why then go looking for them? He might have avoided any thoughts of his family in Canaan by keeping busy in Egypt. He had a wife and children—no sense crying over spilt milk.

The good times were a recent memory because they were only two years into the famine after seven years of plenty. Pharaoh had unprecedented power and wealth, and because of Joseph's diligence, the nations had access to food. "Moreover, all the earth came to Egypt to Joseph to buy grain, because the famine was severe over all the earth" (Gen. 41:57).

But Joseph's past roared into his new life. God was bringing the family back together. Sometimes, leaving things alone isn't enough. What God wants is wholeness and health. The New Testament reminds us that if Jesus is Lord, then if there are conflicts between brothers and sisters, we should work to find healing and wholeness. God isn't just content to graft us into his family. He also wants to teach us what it means to be healthy relationally.

Looked At, But Not Seen

And Joseph's brothers came and bowed themselves before him with their faces to the ground. Joseph saw his brothers and recognized them, but he treated them like strangers and spoke roughly to them. "Where do you come from?" he said. They said, "From the land of Canaan, to buy food." And Joseph recognized his brothers, but they did not recognize him. And Joseph remembered the dreams that he had dreamed of them. . . . And he put them all together in custody for three days.

On the third day Joseph said to them, "Do this and you will live, for I fear God: if you are honest men, let one of your brothers remain confined where you are in custody, and let the rest go and carry grain for the famine of your households, and bring your youngest brother to me. So your words will be verified, and you shall not die." And they did so. Then they said to one another, "In truth we are guilty concerning our brother, in that we saw the distress of his soul, when he begged us and we did not listen. That is why this distress has come upon us." And Reuben answered them, "Did I not tell you not to sin against the boy? But you did not listen. So now there comes a reckoning for his blood." They did not know that Joseph understood them, for there was an interpreter between them. Then he turned away from them and wept. (Gen. 42:6b–24a)

Note first that Joseph "*remembered the dreams that he had dreamed of them [his family]*." Even as Joseph moved on with a new life, he had a nagging thought that one day he might see them again. In his dreams, he imagined the moment. Deep down in his subconscious, there was probably a part of him that wondered what would happen if they ever were reunited. Would they be in shock? Would they run away? Would they embrace him? How would he feel?—Relieved, angry, conflicted? And then one day it happened. Imagination became a reality. In front of him stood nearly all of his brothers. And what happened?

Nothing. Joseph's brothers didn't recognize him. The account is *specific*. He knew them, but they didn't recognize him. He remembered their faces. They seemed to have forgotten his. They looked at him and didn't see him.

Joseph's memories came back with a sharp edge. He faced a rush of emotions. He grew irritable and "spoke roughly." That meant he was terse. He created an accusation to reflect on what to do with this sudden family reunion.

To buy time, he penned them up. He wanted them to think about who they had just met. Maybe some time in reflection would jar a memory loose. He wanted them to consider his voice. He wanted them to remember him. Note that he gave them clues. He told them he feared God, "*for I fear God*." Not the gods of Egypt. There weren't many monotheistic people at that time and in that region. But nothing. They noticed nothing.

During the three days of waiting they wondered what was happening, Joseph was thinking. I like to think he was praying, too. When he spoke next, his tone was more positive. He was more deliberate. At first, he was irritated by the situation in general. After three days, he was reasonable and provided them assurance. God had been working on him.

"Remember the lessons from the bottom of life, Joseph. Remember, it's not about you. Have empathy." He listened to them talk in his native language. It wasn't a language he'd spoken openly for many years. He felt a sense of alienation, of being on the outside looking in. He was both a part of them, and apart from them. Once again, Joseph felt alone. He turned away and wept.

Once the tears dried, Joseph developed a plan. The plan was a way he could still bless his father and brothers with grain while also figuring out if they'd changed. Joseph kept Simeon for insurance and told them to get Benjamin. He then went overboard with sending them gifts back home. They returned to Canaan not only with grain, but also with money. If they were the same brothers they once were, they would take the money and run. After all, they're used to leaving brothers (this time, Simeon) behind. If they remained unchanged, Simeon was just the next name on the hit list. If they were different men, they'd return. Joseph would be able to see their character from this test. Remember, our character emerges when we're tested. What would they do? It would take more time to find out.

In the meantime, Simeon was Joseph's "house guest." Simeon was the second oldest brother in the family. Simeon was one of the two brothers who had slaughtered others in the revenge-killing in Shechem mentioned earlier. According to some traditions, Simeon was the most spiteful of the brothers. Some suggest it was he who initially suggested killing Joseph. Simeon was the brother you had to watch. But this time, Simeon would be the one who stayed behind. Simeon was about to get a small taste of what Joseph had endured. He would lose his freedom, though he wouldn't be a slave or be thrown into a pit. Plus, Joseph could check up on Simeon from time to time. Perhaps they might even establish a new relationship.

The Bible then shifted the scene from Joseph and Simeon back to the brothers. The narrative becomes a story told from two sides, which God was slowly bringing together. The brothers were scared after their encounter with the second most powerful man in Egypt. They were also happy for grain, but wondered who would believe they didn't steal it. The money they'd offered for payment returned with them. They talked with their father and told him of the mighty Egyptian's conditions for staying together as a family.

But Jacob couldn't bear to lose another son. First Joseph, then Simeon, and now the potential of losing Benjamin? Forget it. Jacob decided to try and ride out the famine. But it's hard to outwit, outplay, and outlast God.

Reuben offered to do the right thing. He decided that as the oldest, and the leader, he would offer his sons as collateral. "Dad, if I don't bring back our brother, you can kill my children. Seriously. Give me Benjamin. We can go back and make this work. I'll guarantee it. Dad, please listen."

Jacob didn't. He was making decisions out of fear, not out of faith. "We'll ride out the famine. It's bad, but it may stop any day now. Let's just eat, cut our losses (poor Simeon) and move on." But God was unrelenting. The famine "was severe in the land" (Gen. 43:1). They ate all the grain and then grew desperate again. God used their desperation to bring change and healing.

Different, but Unsure

Like Joseph, you too are different from the person you once were. God has done something remarkable in your life. But it may be that old wounds haven't healed, they've simply been ignored. You want to exercise relational wisdom. But how to do this when all you know are old histories and roles?

At the 2019 Hollywood Film Awards, Robert Downey Jr. presented Shia LeBeouf with the Hollywood Breakthrough Screenwriters Award for writing an autobiographical film called *Honey Boy*. Downey called it "the best and bravest film I've seen in years." *Honey Boy* is about a dysfunctional family relationship. During that introduction, Downey expressed his belief that "all art is therapy" and that one scene depicted "dysfunctional family triangulation." No one blinked, and there were no question marks. Psychological language is now mainstream.

"Dysfunctional family triangulation" is also known as the "drama triangle." Publications like the *Sydney Morning Herald* have been referring to this since 2015, but the concept has been around since the 1960s. It was coined and articulated by psychiatrist Dr. Stephen Karpman. It involves three roles embodied within a family or an individual: "victim, persecutor, and rescuer." Essentially, it means people fulfill specific purposes creating dysfunctional patterns of relating based on self-centered needs. To further explain, here's an excerpt from the *Sydney Morning Herald*:

In a recent blog post, *Eat, Pray, Love* author Elizabeth Gilbert spoke of the rescuer role.

"We each tend to fall into one of those three roles habitually. (Nice to meet you, everyone! My name is Liz Gilbert and I'm a Professional Rescuer!)," she says.

As well as being prone to playing out a particular role, it is also common to flail wildly between the three; moving from wounded, vulnerable victim to manipulating, aggressive persecutor (who fears being victimized and so attacks) to martyr.

"It's a hot mess," Gilbert says.

"I've been reading up on this subject all day and recognizing so many dramas from my own history in these behaviors. I can see so many times where I heightened trouble and even invented (or sought out) drama, because of my unresolved emotional pain. Repetition is the real problem here."

Repetition is the problem. We have specific harmful patterns of family behavior into which we get stuck. As long as things are status quo, most merely cope as best as they can. But what happens when someone in a family is no longer seeking self, but seeking God? What happens to the dynamic when someone is radically changed from the inside out?

Joseph does a few things in this story that can reach across the expanse of time to help us today. No, you don't live in Egypt. No, there's not a famine that requires us to obtain food from another country. There's likely not a massive positional power dynamic that has changed in your life. But there are some lessons to be gleaned that are startlingly contemporary.

Lessons for Renegotiating Relationships

1. Remember that God is at work in and through more people than just you.

It's not just about you. Whenever the past rushes up to us, the first thought is, *They haven't changed.* We assume others are static while we're dynamic. But that's not always the case.

In the story of family reconciliation, keep in mind the possibility that Joseph's brothers are also walking wounded. They not only kept a horrible family secret (selling their brother into slavery), but they also had character issues and incidents with which to contend. For example, God worked in Judah's life to teach him the value of integrity. The man who used to lie to make a quick buck wasn't as quick to lie anymore. The Bible doesn't give us all of the ways God was at work in Joseph's family during his absence, but it gives us enough to realize that he hadn't abandoned them. God was still instructing, guiding, and shaping them individually and collectively.

Often in family dynamics, our first assumption is that the only person wrestling through change is us. Sometimes, it appears that way. If the others were discontent, they would change things, right? To change, we must want to change. Imagine how sad it would be to live an entire life without changing as a person! But sometimes, people simply don't know how to break out of the spiral in which they find themselves.

For example, some siblings tease other family members because they aren't sure how to give a compliment without sounding cheesy or being dismissed. A daughter who might berate her parents even as she is there for every family holiday may do so because she's trying to show she cares. But her parents dread the visit because she makes life miserable. Dysfunctional people want you to understand their longing and take what they say seriously unless, of course, they don't mean what they say. Then they want others to ignore or forgive what they said. No wonder the people around them are in a world of confusion!

Sometimes, God uses circumstances to instigate or generate the changes we need to make. In this story, God used a famine. God can do that. He uses moments of desperation, where we become so desperate for change that we'll do anything to find it. Don't undervalue desperation in the lives of others. Desperate people are often people willing to make changes and seek out solutions. Desperation can break habits and patterns, driving us to our knees because all of the other options are no longer there. The prodigal son was desperate, and that drove him back to his father. Jacob and his sons were desperate, and that drove them to Egypt.

As you renegotiate relationships, it's helpful to think about who is in the conversation. It is not just you and the other person(s). It's you, others, and God. Assuming and imagining the worst can be as deceptive as assuming and imagining the best. The truth is that you simply don't know who is different and how. Begin with a neutral perspective. That doesn't mean it won't hurt. Joseph wept. But it does mean that in your interaction, you can keep the door ajar to more possibilities than the predictive behaviors you once knew.

So often, when families come together, old dynamics reemerge. So often I hear phrases like, "he says he's changed, but I know him" or "she's doing this now, but I know who she is." The assumption is that the people we grew up with or once knew are the same today. Yet, people are dynamic. We're all changing.

2. Choose to respond rather than react.

Though you are now different, old feelings will likely spring up again. It's amazing what our heart remembers about feeling hurt. But because you are different, those hurts need not dictate your response. You know better.

Joseph saw his brothers and had a choice. He could have immediately revealed to them who he was. Instead, he waited. Joseph took the time to respond. We sometimes forget that Christ frees us from the impulses under which we once lived. People listening to Jesus once asked him, "How is it that you say, 'You will become free'?" Jesus answered them, "Truly, truly, I say to you, everyone who practices sin is a slave to sin. The slave does not remain in the house forever; the son remains forever. So, if the Son sets you free, you will be free indeed" (John 8:33–36). Notice that Jesus emphasizes anyone "who practices sin." We're all sinful. We all need a Savior. From what are we set free? Jesus sets us free from being obligated to the sinful response. We have a resurrection power to behave differently than we once did.

So, how do we tell if someone's changed or not? How do we know if the rescuer, victim, or persecutor roles are still in play? Joseph faced this same dilemma. Were his brothers different, or were they the same people they once were? Joseph needed to find out. And as painful and poignant as Joseph felt by going unrecognized by his brothers, this afforded him a window of opportunity to *reflect* and *consider* the best way forward.

A few years ago, I was visiting German relatives over lunch on my birthday. Family members were telling jokes, and I wanted to be funny, too. I started telling a joke without thinking about what the punchline was or where I heard it. I was halfway through it when I realized the joke wasn't appropriate. And because I was translating it from English in my mind, I soon realized it wouldn't translate well either. I was heading for a social cliff and couldn't seem to stop my mouth from throwing me over! After stumbling through the joke (complete with embarrassed laughter and awkwardness afterward), I left lunch to drive four hours to visit friends in northern Germany. The drive allowed me some time to think and reflect. How I wished I'd paused instead of reacting out of my insecurity to share that joke! Taking time to reflect and consider what should be said or done is vital in moving forward toward a better response.

In Christ, each of us has the freedom to respond rather than react. Your feelings may be hurt. You might find old resentments or inferiority complexes rise to the surface. When that happens, take a moment for yourself. Go to a bathroom. Walk around the block. Take some time to pray and reflect. Remember, you're not beholden to your old responses. That doesn't mean others have changed, but it will remind you that you have.

3. Provide an opportunity for others to take personal responsibility.

Joseph used the next seventy-two hours wisely. He was shaken up, but he'd taken some time to calm down. Now he had to figure out if they'd changed and how. Rather than engaging them immediately, he devised a way that allowed them to return home, and then listened in on their response. Our lesson here is to be wise in reengaging emotionally and socially, regardless of our longing for healing and hope. Don't let your hunger for health cloud your judgment. Assess the situation. Joseph's test is simple:

On the third day Joseph said to them, "Do this and you will live, for I fear God: if you are honest men, let one of your brothers remain confined where you are in custody, and let the rest go and carry grain for the famine of your households, and bring your youngest brother to me. So your words will be verified, and you shall not die." And they did so. (Gen. 42:18–20)

Joseph told himself, "I love God first and want to bless my family. They're obviously hungry, and I have the grain. This will be their test of character. I'll keep one of them. The rest I'll send back to get Benjamin. If they leave Simeon behind (who I remember as being callous and hard to love), then I'll know they haven't changed at all. But if they come back with Ben, then I'll know they're no longer the opportunistic, jealous, petty people they once were. I'll see they've matured and value others over their own bruised egos. I'll know that things have changed." In essence, Joseph decided he would provide them a choice and that he would bless them.

Choices reveal desires. Healthy people take responsibility for themselves and others by owning the consequences of their own poor choices. In a typical Twelve–Step program, the important first step begins with an admission of responsibility. "I am an alcoholic." Dysfunctional people either ignore their own poor choices or blame their poor decisions on others. "I didn't mean to yell, but he/she made me do it!" The reality is no one forced them to do anything. They chose to yell.

Now and then, reports of a death row inmate coming to faith in Jesus surfaces. How do you determine if that conversion is real or only for appearances? Here's a good rule of thumb: If the inmate uses their conversion as a basis for an appeal ("I'm now a Christian, let me out"), it's probably manipulative. If they proclaim their conversion while also taking responsibility for the consequences, it's probably genuine. To "demand mercy" undercuts the point of mercy. Mercy can be requested but should never be demanded. Likewise, grace or forgiveness should not be commanded. Some people like to invoke the grace card. "You're a Christian, so you have to show me grace!" But if grace is expected, it ceases to be grace!

We have to take personal responsibility. The determinist says they have no choice, so they aren't accountable. Their actions are the by-products of math. The Christian also believes that God has a purpose, but purpose does not need to negate free will. Christians believe in free will. We have the freedom to choose. If we sow bad seeds, we reap bad crops. If we sow good seeds, we reap good crops (Gal. 6:7–9). Personal responsibility in relationships is key to relational health. Joseph gave his brothers a task to determine a) if they were responsible, and b) toward what or whom they felt a responsibility.

You might be in a friendship where you always have to initiate scheduling time to spend together. Next time be generous to spend that time together but put the ball for scheduling the next meeting in the other person's court. Determine if they volley back. Healthy relationships are two-way streets.

Joseph also blessed them. He made that choice because of who he was as a person. This was not a method of manipulation because he didn't have to bless them as a part of the test. It's okay to test personal responsibility in the relationships around you. Just don't make it so self-serving that you forget to be a blessing to others. The former says something about them, and the latter says something about you. Joseph loaded them down with grain and sent them back with the money initially meant to pay for that grain. But he did not do so frivolously, out of insecurity, or out of a need to be heard.

It's okay to weep and mourn. Joseph wept. Oddly, his professional and personal life were never better. He was at the pinnacle of his career with a family and children who loved him. He employed servants and staff who admired him. But inwardly and suddenly, his heart broke open wide. Just because things appear successful doesn't mean there's no room for hurt. Robin Williams was wildly successful but struggled with depression until his untimely suicide.

Our existential condition always colors our physical circumstances. If you've ever been lonely in a crowded room, you know that the loneliness colors how you view the experience of being in a crowd. Being alone and being lonely are two different things. Jesus talked about these two simultaneous realities all the time. He spoke of this world and the kingdom of God. And he said we could be "near" the kingdom of God, but not be "in" the kingdom of God. Lonely in a crowded room: these two conditions are very much apart, and they are not equal. The loneliness colors how we move and relate to the crowd. What keeps the existential reality from overwhelming us? The answer lies in who else is Lord of that existential space. Jesus can reach through the group into our loneliness. He can bridge worlds. But we need to invite him there.

It is in that place that our brokenness finds a voice and a way to move through it toward healing. Henri Nouwen wrote, "With every loss, there are choices. You choose to live your losses as passages to anger, blame and resentment, or as passages to something new and deeper. The question is not how to avoid loss but how to choose it as a passage, as an exodus to greater life and freedom." What we often do is externalize our hurt toward others to inflict pain. Our existential wounds become the drivers to wound others. In doing so, we find a cycle perpetuated, and wounding becomes a way of relating. And it's perilous when we fall into that pattern because we start to lose sight of how to relate healthily.

We must learn to be honest about our emotional pain without lashing out against others to inflict pain. One meme I recently read said, "Your triggers are your responsibility. It isn't everyone else's obligation to tiptoe around your various moods." Joseph wept. But he didn't tear into his brothers by re-opening every scar that was semi-closed. Instead, he'd experienced God in the dark. He remembered the lesson he'd picked up in prison earlier. That was his motive for blessing.

APPLICATION

1. How are you spending time determining what may or may not be changing in your family dynamics?
2. Are you emotionally inflicting pain on others as a reaction to your desire for change? If so, what ways can you weep without inflicting pain?
3. Are you trying to control outcomes, or are you comfortable trusting God in the waiting?
4. How are you learning not to worry about that which you can't control?
5. What small or big steps are you taking to reintroduce yourself to others? How does the "new you" look?
6. Where do you need some distance to observe unhealthy patterns of relationships without getting caught up in them? How can that alienate you, and are you comfortable with not joining in?

Forgiving and Wisdom

"A family is a place where principles are hammered and honed on the anvil of everyday living." —Charles R. Swindoll

"And he kissed all his brothers and wept upon them. After that his brothers talked with him." —Genesis 45:15

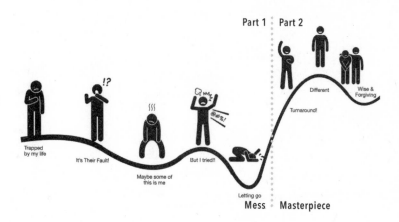

How do we find wisdom as we move in the direction of forgiveness and healing? Forgiving will be an ongoing feature of your life. It's not just past tense, but present tense. Being a forgiving person isn't the same thing as being a gullible person. But without wisdom, it can be.

In the last chapter, we saw how Joseph behaved differently, even though his past ran into his life like a rogue ostrich. He made a choice to bless, but also a choice to test. The test came in the form of holding his brother Simeon, to determine what kind of personal responsibility and care his brothers may or may not have. In the last chapter, a different Joseph determined how different his brothers were. In this chapter, he has to determine how to reunite with them. Maybe that's you, too. You've provided opportunities for others to show they've changed. And now you're either waiting on them or trying to determine how to respond once they've shown they have. It's new territory, and you don't want to charge forward if it's not real. No one wants to be duped.

The Wisdom of Joseph

It took some time for the brothers to return. Joseph didn't know why. From Egypt, he only knew that it was taking them a long time and that they might not return with Benjamin at all. For the second most powerful man in Egypt, there were options open. Joseph could have sent Egyptian spies to see where his family was and what they were doing. He could have spent time working himself into a frenzy when the spies returned with reports saying, "No one is packing. They're just eating the food you gave them." So often, we try to determine the health of the relationships around us and then try to control outcomes based on our desires.

But Joseph waited with Simeon. Simeon must have wondered if his family would come back for him. There is power in waiting. Joseph knew how to wait. This was drilled into him in a pit and in a prison.

Conversely, Joseph learned the power of trust. He could trust God for any outcome. If his brothers returned, Joseph trusted God. If he never saw them again, Joseph trusted God. Be careful of the tendency to be a control freak. We love to provide the guise of choice while secretly working to determine the outcome of that choice.

Maybe your children are going to school, and you've provided them with the tools to take personal responsibility for their choices. Now you're facing the difficulty of trusting God for the outcome. Stop trying to control the outcome. A part of the parenting process is allowing your children to take responsibility for their own choices. Don't give them the illusion of choice. The temptation is to become the kind of parent that hovers. You've told your son or daughter to call their teachers, schedule their classes, or prepare for their job interviews. But then you're tempted to do it for them because you want to help them. But you need to stop because you're not helping them. You're perpetuating a relationship dynamic that isn't good for either of you.

Scholar and psychologist Angela Duckworth wrote the book *Grit: The Power of Passion and Perseverance*. She says, "How often do people start down a path and then give up on it entirely? How many treadmills, exercise bikes, and weight sets are at this very moment gathering dust in basements across the country? How many kids go out for a sport and then quit even before the season is over? How many of us vow to knit sweaters for all of our friends but only manage half a sleeve before putting down the needles? Ditto for home vegetable gardens, compost bins, and diets. How many of us start something new, full of excitement and good intentions, and then give up—permanently—when we encounter the first real obstacle, the first long plateau in progress? Many of us, it seems, quit what we start far too early and far too often. Even more than the effort a gritty person puts in on a single day, what matters is that they wake up the next day, and the next, ready to get on that treadmill and keep going."

Translation: if you're not allowing others to push through their obstacles, you're not helping. Trusting God with the outcome means that you're willing for others to take responsibility without you controlling whether they take said responsibility. That also means you have to be willing to stick with the consequences. Joseph was prepared to hold Simeon indefinitely. I'm sure at times it felt as if he would have to.

They arose and went down to Egypt and stood before Joseph. When Joseph saw Benjamin with them, he said to the steward of his house, "Bring the men into the house, and slaughter an animal and make ready, for the men are to dine with me at noon."

. . . When Joseph came home, they brought into the house to him the present that they had with them and bowed down to him to the ground. And he inquired about their welfare and said, "Is your father well, the old man of whom you spoke? Is he still alive?" They said, "Your servant our father is well; he is still alive." And they bowed their heads and prostrated themselves. And he lifted up his eyes and saw his brother Benjamin, his mother's son, and said, "Is this your youngest brother, of whom you spoke to me? God be gracious to you, my son!" Then Joseph hurried out, for his compassion grew warm for his brother, and he sought a place to weep. And he entered his chamber and wept there. Then he washed his face and came out. And controlling himself he said, "Serve the food." They served him by himself, and them by themselves, and the Egyptians who ate with him by themselves, because the Egyptians could not eat with the Hebrews, for that is an abomination to the Egyptians. And they sat before him, the firstborn according to his birthright and the youngest according to his youth. And the men looked at one another in amazement. Portions were taken to them from Joseph's table, but Benjamin's portion was five times as much as any of theirs. And they drank and were merry with him. (Gen. 43:15b–34)

Thankfully, Joseph's brothers returned to Egypt. They were willing to return for Simeon, and now Joseph had to decide what was next. It's not easy to decide what's next. Joseph had to figure out a way to reintroduce himself. How could he do this without 1) reverting to being the person he used to be, and 2), assuming that just because his brothers accepted personal responsibility, they weren't merely driven by desperation for more food? There were a lot of tears in Joseph's decision. Navigating family messes is an emotional process.

Joseph's brothers returned with Benjamin, money, and gifts. They were honest and open. They said, "the money we came to pay you with last time wound up in our bags on the way back. We have no idea how it got there, so we brought that money back along with more money." Jacob and his sons had a history of lying. Full disclosure was something new.

Joseph reassured them and threw a massive lunch in their honor. At the banquet, he saw Benjamin again for the first time, and this overwhelmed him. He recused himself, wept, and returned ready for the meal.

The story is specific regarding segregation at the banquet because culturally, not only did Egyptians and Semites not mix, but the upper class and lower class didn't sit together. Joseph sat at a separate table in front of his brothers. His servants sat them according to their age. Even the brothers were amazed at how rare an occasion it was to eat together. Benjamin received special treatment, because he was Joseph's full brother. Joseph didn't know if, in his absence, Benjamin had been suffering through the alienation he'd endured.

As they were eating, Joseph figured out another way to test his brothers again while also potentially keeping his youngest brother with him. At first glance, it appears to the reader as if Joseph is cruel to Benjamin by setting him up. Why pick on Ben? The answer is if things went poorly, he wanted the two sons of Rachel to be together. Rachel died giving birth to Benjamin. Joseph was the older of the two and was the only one with a likely memory of his mother. He'd probably spent many nights as a boy longing for his deceased mother to be there. Benjamin was all he had left of her. Of the twelve, it made sense that the two full brothers stick together. Joseph's plan involved trickery and false accusations. It also included a little payback.

This leads us to the most uncomfortable moment in the story. Joseph intended to scare his brothers. He deceived and lied to do it. He planted evidence and then pretended he didn't. Scripture does not approve of Joseph's scheme, but neither does it condemn it. What we know for sure is that God hates lying (Prov. 12:22) and commanded his people against it (Exod. 20:16).

> Then he commanded the steward of his house, "Fill the men's sacks with food, as much as they can carry, and put each man's money in the mouth of his sack, and put my cup, the silver cup, in the mouth of the sack of the youngest, with his money for the grain." And he did as Joseph told him.
>
> As soon as the morning was light, the men were sent away with their donkeys. They had gone only a short distance from the city. Now Joseph said to his steward, "Up, follow after the men, and when you overtake them, say to them, 'Why have you repaid evil for good? Is it not from this that my lord drinks, and by this that he practices divination? You have done evil in doing this.'"

When he overtook them, he spoke to them these words. They said to him, "Why does my lord speak such words as these? Far be it from your servants to do such a thing! Behold, the money that we found in the mouths of our sacks we brought back to you from the land of Canaan. How then could we steal silver or gold from your lord's house? Whichever of your servants is found with it shall die, and we also will be my lord's servants." He said, "Let it be as you say: he who is found with it shall be my servant, and the rest of you shall be innocent." Then each man quickly lowered his sack to the ground, and each man opened his sack. And he searched, beginning with the eldest and ending with the youngest. And the cup was found in Benjamin's sack. Then they tore their clothes, and every man loaded his donkey, and they returned to the city.

When Judah and his brothers came to Joseph's house, he was still there. They fell before him to the ground. Joseph said to them, "What deed is this that you have done? Do you not know that a man like me can indeed practice divination?" (Gen. 44:1–15)

Joseph had a plan, although he didn't need one. He was the second most powerful man around. His brothers were in his hands, and he could have simply taken what he wanted. Hebrews in the land of Canaan were no threat to Egypt. He owed his brothers nothing. But Joseph was a man of integrity and fairness. At heart, he wasn't a liar, a cheat, or an abuser of power.

Yet, he behaved questionably. First, he lulled his brothers into a sense of security. Then he set them up for failure. Like a cop planting evidence in search of a guilty verdict, Joseph manufactured a crime. Perhaps he wanted them to feel as he once did, trapped by circumstances and accused unfairly. We can only speculate.

His brothers were frightened. They believed one of them would die, and the others would be taken captive. The steward's search was methodical and deliberate, beginning with the eldest and moving to the youngest. It was excruciatingly slow, until Benjamin was found with the cup. The men "tore their clothes" (which is the Bible's way of saying they were frustrated, afraid, and anxious), and trekked back to the city. The brothers were right to worry. Stealing from royalty was a capital offense. And association with the thief carried guaranteed consequences. Every step seemed certain death or imprisonment.

It was the steward, not Joseph, who heard their pleas of innocence. They returned to Joseph's house, and Joseph asked them an accusatory question. He then deceived them by telling them a man like him practiced divination. Divination is the power to see by supernatural means. It's not technically a lie. Joseph didn't claim *he* had the power of clairvoyance. His claim was that the typical Egyptian in his position practiced divination. And that was true. Joseph's steward also never said Benjamin would die. He said that Benjamin would become Joseph's servant, and the other brothers would be declared innocent. It was a scripted response and, in retrospect, must have been a curious one. It didn't follow what the brothers knew was common practice, staggering in its leniency.

Joseph aimed to keep Benjamin without casting blame on his brothers. If the brothers returned without Benjamin, they could honestly tell their father that it was Ben's fault. They would not be to blame. So, Joseph's ploy was not designed primarily to torture the brothers. It was designed to give them maximum deniability while also moving Benjamin away from what he assumed was still a toxic situation. But as much as we want to admire his cunning, it's confusing to see a man of such integrity take this tack.

What happened next was surprising and unexpected. When Joseph accused his brother Benjamin of stealing, Judah stepped in. He did so with eloquence and grace.

And Judah said, "What shall we say to my lord? What shall we speak? Or how can we clear ourselves? God has found out the guilt of your servants; behold, we are my lord's servants, both we and he also in whose hand the cup has been found." (Gen. 43:16)

Joseph's plan backfired. He didn't expect all of the brothers to pledge themselves as servants to him in solidarity with Benjamin. He knew they had families. He'd listened to their conversation over dinner the previous evening. He told them that only Benjamin would stay with him. Benjamin was the one he was trying to save. They could "go up in peace" back to Jacob (Gen. 43:17).

But remember, God had been working in this family during Joseph's absence. In one sense, Judah reintroduced Joseph's family to Joseph. Joseph thought he knew how his brothers would behave. He based this on family history. But Judah would show Joseph they had changed too.

Others May Be Different Too

Then Judah went up to him and said, "Oh, my lord, please let your servant speak a word in my lord's ears, and let not your anger burn against your servant, for you are like Pharaoh himself. . . .

"For your servant became a pledge of safety for the boy to my father, saying, 'If I do not bring him back to you, then I shall bear the blame before my father all my life.' Now therefore, please let your servant remain instead of the boy as a servant to my lord, and let the boy go back with his brothers. For how can I go back to my father if the boy is not with me? I fear to see the evil that would find my father." (Gen. 43:18–34)

Note that it's Judah and not Reuben. You'll recall that in Genesis 42:37–38 it was Reuben who offered his sons as collateral if he didn't bring Benjamin and Simeon back safely. But when the moment arrived, it was Judah who spoke, and he spoke the truth. Lies had destroyed Judah's family. Judah was so sick of lies he refused to lie again. Schemes or trickery were no longer tools to advance his agenda. Judah decided the truth is his best option. Judah had changed.

Judah's approach in talking with this powerful Egyptian ruler—a man he does not yet recognize as his brother—is refreshingly open. In his brief speech, he admitted that Benjamin was all Jacob had of his *favorite* wife's sons. He told the ruler of the story of how it would break his father's heart if he lost both sons. Judah decided he would "bear the blame before my father all my life" if he didn't bring Benjamin back safely. Judah was determined to treat Benjamin differently than he did Joseph. And Judah did one more thing: he offered himself up in Benjamin's place. Perhaps he wished he'd done the same with Joseph.

Imagine what that was like to hear from Joseph's perspective. When Judah said, "His [Benjamin's] brother is dead" Joseph didn't stop to probe. He didn't interrupt and say, "You jerk! That brother wasn't dead. He was sold to a caravan of Ishmaelites!" He didn't make this moment about him. Instead, he simply listened. It's so hard to listen when you have so much you want to say. But Joseph had learned to listen to prisoners as he cared for them, even as he listened to God's promises and reassurances. Joseph listened for God to speak, even as Judah was speaking.

Joseph: The Art of Forgiving

There comes a moment in our lives where we have to make a decision. Will we forgive or not forgive? Forgiveness is an act between myself and God that essentially states, *The past will no longer hold sway over me. I'm accepting a change and letting its power over me go.*

Miroslav Volf said that sometimes we "forgive in droplets." Sometimes forgiveness comes little by little. At other times, forgiveness comes in a wave. Forgiving does just as much for the forgiver as the one(s) forgiven. In letting go of the offenses against you, you allow for healing to reside in the wounds of bitterness or resentment. That healing allows for some closure.

> Then Joseph could not control himself before all those who stood by him. He cried, "Make everyone go out from me." So no one stayed with him when Joseph made himself known to his brothers. And he wept aloud, so that the Egyptians heard it, and the household of Pharaoh heard it. And Joseph said to his brothers, "I am Joseph! Is my father still alive?" But his brothers could not answer him, for they were dismayed at his presence.

So Joseph said to his brothers, "Come near to me, please." And they came near. And he said, "I am your brother, Joseph, whom you sold into Egypt. And now do not be distressed or angry with yourselves because you sold me here, for God sent me before you to preserve life. For the famine has been in the land these two years, and there are yet five years in which there will be neither plowing nor harvest. And God sent me before you to preserve for you a remnant on earth, and to keep alive for you many survivors. So it was not you who sent me here, but God. He has made me a father to Pharaoh, and lord of all his house and ruler over all the land of Egypt. Hurry and go up to my father and say to him, 'Thus says your son Joseph, God has made me lord of all Egypt. Come down to me; do not tarry. You shall dwell in the land of Goshen, and you shall be near me, you and your children and your children's children, and your flocks, your herds, and all that you have. There I will provide for you, for there are yet five years of famine to come, so that you and your household, and all that you have, do not come to poverty.' And now your eyes see, and the eyes of my brother Benjamin see, that it is my mouth that speaks to you. You must tell my father of all my honor in Egypt, and of all that you have seen. Hurry and bring my father down here." Then he fell upon his brother Benjamin's neck and wept, and Benjamin wept upon his neck. And he kissed all his brothers and wept upon them. After that his brothers talked with him. (Gen. 45:1–15)

This is a beautiful moment. There are five things Joseph did that are worth highlighting. First, when Joseph reintroduced himself to his brothers, he made sure he chose the environment. When you talk about who you are or how you've changed, be sure to protect your moment. Decide who will be in the room. The Egyptians weren't in the room.

Years ago, I asked my father what I thought was a good accountability question. His reaction stunned me. He raised his voice and yelled at me on our front lawn through tears streaming down his face. Our relationship up to that point was good, so I was stunned. Six months later, when Dad decided to talk with me again, he said it was because others were in the room when I asked. It didn't matter that they weren't paying attention and didn't hear me ask. He was embarrassed by the question and made the assumption they'd heard. I'd neglected to choose the environment wisely.

Second, Joseph was heartfelt and genuine in his response. He wept. He said, "I am Joseph!" In fact, he was loud about it. The "household of Pharaoh" heard it even though it was a private moment between them. But this wasn't performance art, and Joseph wasn't putting on an emotional production. He was transparent. When the right people are in the right place, be as authentic and honest as you possibly can. This requires a moment of vulnerability and faith. It's a risk. But courage at the right moments tends to reap the rewards.

Third, Joseph didn't make this moment about himself. In his transparency, his first thought was to ask about Jacob, his father. His brothers were taken aback. They didn't answer because they were "dismayed at his presence." That means they were really, really scared. They had no idea where this is going. They were unsure what would happen next. Joseph, the brother they thought was removed from their lives forever, was the second most powerful man in Egypt. There he stood, dressed as an Egyptian, and they hadn't recognized him. Their collective heads must have been spinning. But Joseph didn't grow angry. Instead, he began to explain his journey and God's purposes.

Fourth, Joseph kept the focus on what God is doing. Consider what he said:

- God sent me before you to preserve life.
- So, it was not you who sent me here, but God.
- He [God] has made me a father to Pharaoh.
- God has made me lord of all Egypt.

Who *didn't* he blame? Not once did Joseph blame his brothers. He didn't scold them or call them names. He didn't tell them they'd hurt his feelings (and they very clearly did). Joseph had a higher perspective. His focus wasn't on his family. His focus was on God at work in and through him to bless others.

Fifth, his tone was hopeful and positive. Joseph's tone was different from his tone of years before when he was a teenager. Remember when he first had a dream and told his father and brothers they would bow down before him? He didn't bring that up. Joseph didn't use this moment to say, *See, I told you so!*

More importantly, he didn't frame what had happened as a way of reminding them who was in charge. Instead, Joseph focused on why. In reintroducing your new self to others, it's essential you reframe the *tone* of your relationship. Most people remember the tenor of a relationship and then retrofit the facts to the tenor they perceive. In his brothers' minds, Joseph had been arrogant and lacked empathy. As Joseph explained how God had brought him through, his humility and concern for others shone through. The old self was self-centered. The new was selfless. It chose grace at the moment where it was easy to be ungracious. But graciousness does not mean forgetfulness. We sometimes confuse graciousness with amnesia. Mercy embraces the past as a part of the redemption of the future. It does not ignore it.

Lessons for Wisdom and Forgiveness

1. Allow others to reintroduce themselves to you and be ready to reintroduce yourself to them.

Exercise wisdom in trusting God for the timing of others to demonstrate to you what may or may not have changed. In reconciliation, it's important to listen fully. Allow the other person to reintroduce themselves to you. It just might give you an opportunity to reintroduce yourself to them. Conversely, their responses in opportunities to take personal responsibility may tell you the moment isn't yet right. Embrace patience in the process. Provide opportunities for others to step into a divine opportunity. Then listen carefully for what's changed. Remember, they need to reintroduce themselves to you and you to them. Exercise some caution in the process as well. Joseph didn't reveal who he was to them until he was certain there was a change of heart. Don't force conversations that aren't ready to happen. Step into the conversation when the wisdom you're exercising begins to pay off. And remember, you'll need to be transparent at some point. When you arrive at that moment, follow the example of Joseph: don't make it all about you. That "old self insecurity" might be what they're listening for as well.

2. Celebrate and ceremonialize the moment.

In 2016, my father was killed instantly by a driver while riding his bicycle in the early morning. My sister called me from North Carolina and told me what had happened. I quickly hopped on a plane. It seemed the end of an era. We'd buried our mother in 2009. Suddenly, all my sister and I had were memories.

Deaths of loved ones are complicated for family. I've seen families fight and divide after a death. The division of stuff—down to who gets the dining room chairs—can create rifts in families that never close. My sister and I, however, found a way to celebrate even beyond the emotional memorial service. We decided we would not fight over anything. Decisions became opportunities to come together, to talk about what we missed and what we wanted. Our families drew closer. What could have been a moment to tear us apart brought us together. The year after Dad's death, we went on a memorial bike ride. How you celebrate is a way of building culture.

Joseph and his brothers celebrated a miraculous reunion. They threw a party. There was a commotion. Pharaoh himself heard about the party and rewarded Joseph's re-found family.

"Then he fell upon his brother Benjamin's neck and wept, and Benjamin wept upon his neck. And he kissed all his brothers and wept upon them. After that his brothers talked with him. When the report was heard in Pharaoh's house, 'Joseph's brothers have come,' it pleased Pharaoh and his servants" (Gen. 45:14–16).

They decided to relocate to Egypt. Joseph let everyone go back, including Benjamin, to pack the moving camels. He was now operating solely on trust. He didn't fully know if they would return. They had, after all, everything they wanted and more. But Joseph was willing to take this leap of faith. It's easier to trust others when you're in a healthy relationship. Robert Frost wrote, "The greatest thing in family life is to take a hint when a hint is intended—and not to take a hint when a hint isn't intended." Where there's high trust, you give others the benefit of the doubt. You no longer suspect the worst but ascribe to them the best motives and intentions.

When Joseph and Jacob were reunited, there were more tears. The text is specific that Joseph and Jacob wept "a good while" (Gen. 46:29). But there's another ceremony ahead:

> Then Joseph brought in Jacob his father and stood him before Pharaoh. . . . And Jacob blessed Pharaoh and went out from the presence of Pharaoh. Then Joseph settled his father and his brothers and gave them a possession in the land of Egypt, in the best of the land, in the land of Rameses, as Pharaoh had commanded. And Joseph provided his father, his brothers, and all his father's household with food, according to the number of their dependents. (Gen. 47:5–12)

Israel (Jacob) met Pharaoh, the most important king of the largest empire in that area of the world and blessed him. The text repeats it twice. Israel blessed the nations. This was a ceremony with one the head of a government, and the other the head of God's chosen family. The family blessed the country. And Israel did this personally. Throughout Scripture, followers of Yahweh and Jesus are commanded to bless others. So often, we want the world to bless us. But the blessing is celebrated. It's marked and remembered. When God does something miraculous, it's necessary to memorialize it and remember. Repeat the story over and over. It will be a comfort for you when life becomes difficult again.

3. Don't be complacent—ground your expectations and focus on reality.

Sometimes we read the story of Joseph and think, "It's a Disney ending! Let's watch the end credits roll." But the reality is different. We're all imperfect. Joseph's family was back together, but life marched on. There was still a famine to get through.

Everyone—I mean the whole family—now lived together in a foreign country. I've lived with my family in foreign countries. This presents a whole new level of stress. Though it can also draw you together, it doesn't mean there are no fights or quarrels. Anytime you throw family in-laws (complete with some family outlaws) into the mix, there are bound to be complications.

But things were still complicated. You might think, "They've got it made in the shade! They're family of the second most powerful man in Egypt. They all have food in a famine." In truth, the average Egyptian hated the influx of foreigners. And not only were these foreigners taking the best land, but also their occupation was despised.

> "When Pharaoh calls you and says, 'What is your occupation?' you shall say, 'Your servants have been keepers of livestock from our youth even until now, both we and our fathers,' in order that you may dwell in the land of Goshen, for every shepherd is an abomination to the Egyptians." (Gen. 46:33–34)

Goshen was in lower Egypt, which was full of pastures. It was 650 miles away from Canaan. In Genesis 47:13, we read, "Now there was no food in all the land, for the famine was very severe, so that the land of Egypt and the land of Canaan languished by reason of the famine." Anyone who has moved (and we've moved multiple times) knows how difficult it can be to establish a new rhythm. Suddenly, they had to learn Egyptian to barter. Where they once knew where every cistern was, they would have to learn all over again. Disruption isn't necessarily bad. Sometimes, it can be an opportunity to start over. Even as Joseph and his family began a new chapter, so too the whole family began another chapter on the journey of faith.

If God works through your dysfunctional self and your dysfunctional relationships to create health, he will also establish a new norm. But that does not mean you can afford to be complacent. It means that when the celebration fades, you have to be diligent in staying within the new relational culture that's been established. If we're not careful, relationships can drift. Families can fall back into old dysfunctions or develop new dysfunctions. Everyone involved has to be committed to health.

APPLICATION

1. Which moments in your life would you describe as "redemption stories"?
2. What has to happen for relationships to find healing?
3. How did you notice character change tested in these verses?
4. Joseph's response in 45:4–5 is staggering. He first has to describe who he is and then lets his brothers know he is not seeking vindication. How have you had to explain to others who you are in Christ? In what ways do they not recognize you anymore?
5. It is said that time heals all wounds. But Joseph was weeping. Some wounds cut so deep that time and distance require more. They need God to step in and treat the injury. Which wounds from your past are still fresh? Which are healed? How can or should God step in?

10
Forging a New Life Together

"As a child my family's menu consisted of two choices: take it or leave it."
—Buddy Hackett

∎

"But when they told him all the words of Joseph, which he had said to them, and when he saw the wagons that Joseph had sent to carry him, the spirit of their father Jacob revived." —Genesis 45:27

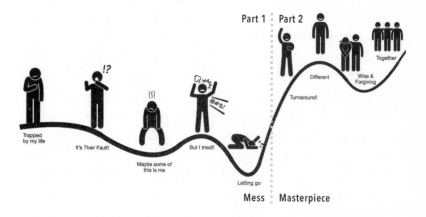

The more familiar society is with something, the more words society has to describe it. Eskimos have fifty words for snow. American English has fifteen. One scientific study on colors and language stated, "We name the colors of things we want to talk about." In other words, we have more descriptive words for things about which we want to talk. One person noted that different cultures have differing numbers of words for colors. The higher the familiarity with something, the more words to describe that something. Today we have a larger therapeutic vocabulary to describe dysfunctional relationships than at any time in history. It seems as if everyone is either in therapy or knows someone in treatment. From attention deficit disorder to schizophrenia, it seems as if new psychosomatic terms roll into our lexicon each day. But just because we can describe dysfunction does not mean we're healthier. Knowing we're sinful is different from doing something about it.

Just when you think that the family story is over, we read this verse from Joseph as he sends his brothers back for their move to Egypt. "Then he [Joseph] sent his brothers away, and as they departed, he said to them, 'Do not quarrel on the way'" (Gen. 45:24). Joseph still felt the need to instruct his brothers not to quarrel. Why? We all tend to slip back into old patterns and habits. And as soon as we find healing in one area of our lives (in this case, a reunited family), other parts of our lives are exposed. We are a never-ending redemption project.

Some believe that dysfunction is just the way things work. Petulance is embraced. One family I know has a family member who can start screaming, accusing, and throwing things on a whim. The family solution is to react, and then afterward to pretend as if the eruption never occurred. They think that if they ignore it, the behavior will go away. Of course, it doesn't. If anything, the individual has learned a social expectation: they can do whatever they want, and without consequences for anything they say or throw. The family has learned to live with the elephant in the room. That's just the way things are. Perhaps you've heard someone say, "We just don't talk about it." The result is an environmental lack of authenticity and honesty. We become caricatures of ourselves, uncertain about how to navigate healthy relationships. We tell ourselves that's just the way things work. But does it have to work that way?

Many parents are so desperate to be their child's best friends that they're willing to facilitate just about anything the child wants. There's a scene in the movie *The Sound of Music* where the character played by Julie Andrews (Maria) sits down for dinner and uses reverse psychology that causes the children to cry. One by one, they leave the dinner table in shame for what they had done to her earlier. Today, some would consider that emotional child abuse. If a child is crying, they believe it is the worst thing in the world. Children should never sob, right? Wrong. Some tears are healthy.

Children today often tell their parents what they need and what they want. The assumption is that children know what's best for them. But anyone who was once a child knows differently. Children aren't always the best judges for what they want or need. As a child, I wanted Twinkies. But that didn't mean I should have them.

The purpose of childhood is discovery. Children need to discover the boundaries of social interaction and even of limitations within themselves. It's their job to push, and it's the parent's job to love them enough to push back appropriately. The term "appropriately" here is critical. Every parent struggles with what is appropriate and when. Grace is required. But so too is resolve.

One *Wall Street Journal* article stated, "Millennials Are the Therapy Generation." I am pro counseling and therapy. I would much rather have someone seek an outside perspective with some expertise than do nothing at all. We all need help from time to time. But therapy was not meant to become perpetual therapy. Treatment is there to help us when we cannot see a way through the storm.

So, what are we to do? Navigating ongoing relationships requires a commitment to new ways of relating. In other words, finding resolution in relationships requires one set of relational skills. Establishing new patterns moving forward requires another. Joseph's family settled in Goshen. But they still had to get along.

Lessons in Togetherness

1. Reinforce a new culture.

Culture is fostered by what you celebrate, and what you celebrate has roots in who you value. A prominent US pastor said the following during a Sunday morning service, "I want to encourage each one of us to realize, when I obey God, I'm not doing it for God. I mean, that's one way to look at it, but we're doing it for ourselves. Because God takes pleasure when we're happy. That's the thing that gives him the greatest joy this morning. So, I want you to know this morning—just do good for your own self. Do good 'cause God wants you to be happy. When you come to church, when you worship him. You're not doing it for God, really. You're doing it for yourself. 'Cause that's what makes God happy."

That sounds appealing, doesn't it? "You're doing it for yourself because that's what makes God happy." But does it?

There's a type of pride that can creep into our hearts. The quote above is the fastest way to disingenuousness in relationships. Yes, God wants what's good for us. But good isn't the same as happy. Eating ice cream for breakfast, lunch, and dinner makes me happy. But it isn't good for me. Carrots and broccoli and peas may sound like suffering, but the ultimate result is health. Humility begins with the desperation that you need God to do in you that which you can't, and the conviction that his pathway to healing is better than your own.

Here's why it matters: if you spend your time celebrating what makes you happy, you'll create a culture of manipulation and distortion. There's nothing wrong with being happy. But the ability to genuinely rejoice in God's best for others creates a culture of selflessness and cohesion.

Culture is fostered by what you celebrate, so you must be very careful in choosing what to highlight. If you celebrate selflessness, you'll create a culture of selflessness. If you celebrate selfishness, you'll develop a culture of selfishness.

We live in the age of the selfie. Everything in a person's life is celebrated, framed, and posted. The challenge is that we believe we're selfless because we participate in others' "look at me, like me, and see that I'm special" need. We feed the beast because starving it seems cruel. People who demand attention should be attended to, right? The squeaky wheel, after all, gets the grease. Isn't it funny, though, how there's never enough grease? Oddly, if we're not careful, a process of manipulation takes over:

- I celebrate you so that you can celebrate how I celebrated you.
- In return, you celebrate me.
- Then I celebrate how you celebrated me, which you both expect and feel you deserve.
- I don't like that you believe you deserve it, especially when I

deserve more attention for all of the ways I gave you attention.

- You don't like that it's about me and are resentful it's not more about you.
- We both stay in the relationship because, while we don't necessarily like each other, we're addicted to the perception of being liked by each other.

And on it goes. But God says that when people are desperate enough for change, the starting point is humility. "If my people who are called by my name will humble themselves, and pray . . . then I will . . . heal their land" (2 Chron. 7:14). Humility doesn't mean we ignore each other. But it does mean applauding moments of genuine selflessness. Healing begins with a humble spirit and prayers that God can do that which we can't. Humility is a bridge between our present and our potential.

What we celebrate has roots in who we value. If we value ourselves, then we honor ourselves. If we value God, then we celebrate God. And when God works in and through us, we learn to encourage each other in life without self-centeredness. There's an old saying, "The family that prays together stays together." This sounds old-fashioned and glib. It is neither.

2. Practice and model courage. Courage is what emerges when obedience to God trumps our need for safety.

Every new parent is worried they'll mess up their kids. New parents believe they'll raise their kids so well there will be no dysfunctionality. They'll do it better than their parents. Though Melissa and I were both healthy, well-adjusted people, we too had a small list of things we thought we could do better than our parents. We believed we would parent better than any parent has ever parented. All we needed to do was follow God and be obedient.

You'd think that obedience means a lack of fear. But that wasn't our experience. God moved us all over the world, and our sons were the new kids over and over again. More frequently than I care to recall, the fears of being rejected by new peoples in new cultures emerged.

Our sons had to make friends in places where no one spoke their mother tongue. Sometimes, they were the only Americans in their entire school! Sometimes, they were the only Christ-followers. And they were in contexts where neither being an American nor a Christian was cool. Over and over again, Melissa and I were genuinely afraid for our children. I was worried that all of the love we had for them would be dismissed or forgotten by the challenges they faced in life.

Then there was the guilt. Joshua 24:15 says, "As for me and my house, we will serve the LORD." We believed that. The children followed the parents. But we also wondered if by following God, we were damaging them.

One day, living overseas in a particularly difficult season, I was torn. I loved my sons so much that when they hurt, I hurt for them. It felt like the weight of the world was on my shoulders. We saw advances and miracles in our context, but I wondered—at what cost? And then, God providentially spoke through an older, wiser missionary couple. In a raw conversation, after I poured my heart out, they said, "God loves your children more than you do."

My heart nearly stopped. This older couple was right! God's capacity to love far outweighed my own. We arrogantly thought that our love was what mattered most. But God's love was what mattered most. If we were in his will, following him faithfully, then he would take the challenges and turn them into blessings for those who follow him. "And we know that for those who love God all things work together for good, for those who are called according to his purpose" (Rom. 8:28). Assurance flooded my soul. Whatever challenges our sons were facing, because we were in the center of his will, God would use those to shape them into the men he wanted them to be (if they would choose to follow him). My sons were developing grit, and grit is needed in life. God would use their unique experiences to bring unique blessings to the world. God would use the unique challenges they were overcoming to bless others in ways exclusive to them.

"Perfect love casts out fear" (1 John 4:18). That doesn't mean you won't be afraid or that there aren't legitimate concerns in life. But it does mean that fear pales in comparison to your love for Jesus. When Jesus was in the Garden of Gethsemane, his perfect love for God overrode his trepidation at the crucifixion he knew was coming. His trust was in the Father. "Father, if you are willing, remove this cup from me. Nevertheless, not my will, but yours, be done" (Lk. 22:42). This didn't mean Jesus was wrong to ask God if it was possible to remove the challenge before him. But his choice to obey was determined. Jesus wanted what the Father wanted.

To rewire new relationships, both parties must have the courage to obey something (or someone) more significant than themselves. Some people establish "new rules" for interacting. Having new rules is a good step. The courage comes with the follow-through. For example, a young couple may have a "rule" that they'll never go to bed angry. That rule sounds easy when you're getting along. But when it's 2 a.m., and you're still not asleep, that rule can be easy to abandon. Rules-based marriages can sound great . . . at first. I know a couple who determined they would split the chores. They kept a running chart on who did the dishes. It seemed so good until one of them had to leave town for a business trip. Then they amended their rule. Over time, one of them grew resentful at the other because the score they were keeping had grown lopsided.

Courage is what emerges when obedience to God trumps our need for safety. In the case of dishes, it's the safety of knowing you're not being cheated by having to do more dishes than the other. For us, it was the safety of staying in one place without having to change our environment. Playing it safe is always a choice. But when compared to courage in obeying God, it's never the best choice.

Safety means avoiding conflict. Obedience to God sometimes means risking conflict to find a resolution. Sometimes, courage is speaking up when you could be quiet.

As I recounted earlier, my dad was killed while he was cycling. The man who hit him had drugs in his system and didn't see him carefully, methodically, and slowly riding on the side of the road. When the car hit him, he flew nearly 80 feet and was internally decapitated. That was a sudden, brutal blow to my sister and me, who already had unexpectedly lost our mother a few years earlier.

The court case dragged on for over a year. I wanted the man to suffer the consequences, but I also wanted to respond as a Christ-follower. The final day in court coincided with the week I was preparing a sermon for Palm Sunday. The district attorney contacted my sister and told her that we could have anything we'd like to have read aloud in the courtroom before the defendant.

I had decided not to respond. Staying quiet was the safe choice. The driver had been silent for months, so I thought he should reap cold silence in return.

But I belong to Jesus. He leads, and I follow. In my heart, I knew he was calling me to have the courage to respond. I wrestled internally, but with an hour to go, I sat down and wrote. Here is what was read in the courtroom:

Today is a day that we've been praying for: justice and consequences for poor actions and grace for all those involved. Not a day has passed since Dad was hit at high velocity and thrown so many feet toward his instant death that I haven't thought of him. My grandchild has since been born. Both of my parents are now dead; my sister and I the only ones left in a house of faith and love. In these passing months, I've had to consistently give a fear I have over to God. The fear is that there would be no regret on the part of the driver. The thought starts to creep in that maybe he's convinced himself that hitting a bicyclist who was slow to pedal and careful in being visible and on the side of a road is somehow okay. I've fought with worries that he's not thought of the life he took and the cost that was paid. Whenever we lose someone we love, it leaves a hole. That's a sign of how much that person loved and was loved. Dad was loved by us. And he loved us. And that has left a hole. But each time those fears and worries come up, I'm grateful that I can give those over to my Lord and Savior, Jesus Christ. He reminds me that He paid the price of giving His life so that I might live. He tells me through the Bible that where I deserved death, He gave me life. So many believe that God isn't real. I once thought the same. I thought that God was the product of the religious culture one was raised in. No one was more surprised than I to discover that God was real. Describing that reality is like trying to describe color to those who see in black and white. How do you describe someone others are convinced isn't real? Maybe this is a moment of disruption. Maybe this is a time where God put everyone in a courthouse so that they can know that God is real, and Jesus is alive. Seems appropriate that this Sunday is Palm Sunday and next Sunday is Easter. He is risen indeed. So, my heart aches, but I do know that Dad gave control of his life to Jesus. And when we give our lives to Jesus, He enters into our lives while we breathe now, and He ushers us into eternity to be with Him. Dad started that morning riding a bike. In an instant, he graduated to a home with Jesus. I'll see him one day. That's my assurance. The question is: will you? Even Dad would hope that you would let Him into your heart. I forgive you not because you deserve it. I forgive you because I was forgiven. And Jesus offers forgiveness to you. You took my dad. But you didn't take him away forever. I miss him every day, but I'll see him again. I am praying for justice, because I think consequences matter. But I'm also praying for forgiveness and grace through Jesus Christ. Thank you.

Courage because of obedience caused my heart to break and forgive that man. When he heard it, my sister told me he broke down and sobbed. He'd wanted to reach out but was told by his lawyer to remain silent. My sister, who was in the courtroom, had a more courageous task. She had to look at him in the eyes. My sister decided before she walked into the courtroom to forgive the man who killed our father. She is a follower of Jesus too.

Moments of courage come to us, moments where obedience to God rubs against our desires for safety. Healthy relationships make for a conscious choice to be courageous.

3. Root your identity: Your worth is established vertically, not horizontally.

Michelle walked into our church offices and asked to meet with a pastor. Michelle sat in the front row each Sunday and had been attending church for about three weeks. As she sat down, she began to tear up. She said, "I've been thinking about what it means to surrender. But I didn't understand what it meant until last Monday. You'd said that God is the author of my book, and I needed to be the author of my own life no longer. Last Monday night I surrendered my life to Jesus." I told her how excited I was for her but saw her smile and look away. I then asked what was wrong. She said, "I've done so many bad things in my life, and ever since making that decision, things have been so good. When does the other shoe drop? I just don't feel like I deserve this." Together, we talked about the difference between "deserve" and" value." No one deserves forgiveness. But that doesn't mean we aren't valuable. The mere fact that out of his immense love for us God sent his Son to die shows us that we hold tremendous value for him. But none of us deserves that love.

This distinction is essential. The language of "self-love" is everywhere, and most of the time, the words are misleading. The person isn't referring to their desperation to love themselves, but to value themselves. We all want to feel worthwhile, which is why one of the deepest wounds an adult can give is to tell someone they're "worthless." This preys on our deepest fears of insignificance. When we feel small, we believe we *are* small.

If we give others the power to determine our worth, we'll chase affirmation by those who wield power but shouldn't. I can't stress enough how difficult this is because we often seek worth from those we shouldn't.

In adolescence, this is one of those things that cause sincere regret. Parents remind their teen how much worth they have, but the teen doesn't listen. Instead, they seek worth by how their peers or teachers view them. Some can receive worth from everyone except one person who refuses to give it. And like a moth to a flame, they'll gravitate toward that person in the hope of gaining value.

In Scripture, Satan tempted Jesus to find his worth in how Satan viewed him. Jesus was tempted to show his power by Satan's demand.

Satan wanted Jesus to want his approval rather than God's approval. Jesus's response was to quote Scripture back to Satan. Why? Was this a glib response or a profound strategy for dealing with the temptation of finding our worth in the approval of others? It was the latter. Jesus quoted Scripture to remind Satan of truth. The father of lies wanted to tempt Jesus into thinking that his worth was in demonstrating his attributes on demand. But Jesus quoted Scriptures to indicate he was not bound to respond when others demanded he do so. Scriptures gave Jesus a reference point for dealing with worth.

When the world wants to convince you that your worth comes from their approval, remember how fickle their support is. In those moments, begin with this fundamental truth: the most infinite, perfect Being ever known believes you are of infinite worth.

Where you find your worth has tremendous implications in your on-going relationships. Finding resolution is one thing. Believing your worth isn't determined by kowtowing to future demands of others is another. When I know my worth to God, I don't allow others to cheapen that worth. Leaving an abusive relationship becomes an issue of stewardship of what God considers worthwhile. If you frame it in terms of self-love, the vocabulary sets you up for loneliness. It's just not that much fun to be alone. But if you have a biblical framework for worth, you know who is with you and why. Your head isn't bowed in shame but rises with the knowledge that God sees more worth in you more than you do.

As I write this, suicide is on the rise globally. Suicide occurs when you believe you are no longer worthwhile. It's a sin because it's a violation of God's very creation of you. He created you because of your worth. He came for you, died, and rose for you because you are his creation, and God does not create worthless human beings. Everyone has the potential to recognize their worth and seize their God-given potential. When we lose sight of who God deems worthy, we begin to evaluate what we or others believe is worthwhile. We're horrible judges of evaluating what's worthwhile.

Don't let others market a lie to you. Scripture establishes the truth and perspective of who you are. When you know that, you're free to act without the need to placate others.

APPLICATION

1. How would you describe the relational culture in which you find yourself? How do you contribute to it? How do you wish it would change? What daily choices can you make to celebrate the right things?

2. How has God called you to show courage? Where are you playing it safe, and how has that hurt you as a person?

3. Sometimes, our longing for wholeness in family relationships leads us to be undiscerning in what we do or how we do it. How can you exercise discernment relationally? What questions, statements, attitudes, or attributes can you foster that will lead to health?

4. How have you struggled with self-worth? Write down ways you think a proper view of self will result in better relationships with others.

11

A New View!

"The riddles of God are more satisfying than the solutions of Man."
—G. K. Chesterton

■

"Jesus answered him, 'What I am doing you do not understand now, but afterward you will understand.'" —John 13:7

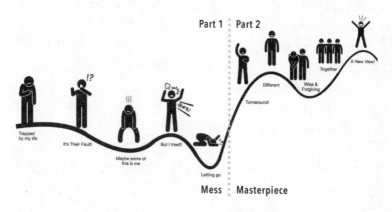

This journey toward wholeness and healing has largely been about your personal journey. Along the way, we've seen that God is at work in others, even as he is working on us. In this penultimate chapter, I want to broaden your perspective and widen your imagination. If you've ever climbed a mountain or a large hill, a part of the purpose is to look out on a new view. It would be a shame to reach a peak and spend the time thinking about where you've been or where you're going without appreciating the beauty and majesty of the vista. If we were explorers, we would climb a rise not only to glimpse the panoramic view, but also to re-align ourselves for the journey back down the mountain as we forge new pathways forward. In short, let's see if we can get a small glimpse of God's masterpiece.

Panoramas

On October 11, 1832, a rice-laden ship carrying a crew of fourteen left the coast of Japan. Otokichi, Kyukichi, and Iwakichi were three of those fourteen. Otokichi was only fourteen years old. The ship ran into a severe storm, and all but those three lost their lives. The boat drifted across the Pacific Ocean and landed in Washington State in the northwest of the United States. By the time they drifted onto Cape Flattery, Otokichi was fifteen and barely clinging to life. The Makah Indians found the three men and fed them because they needed more slaves, and these men might also be traded for goods. The three Japanese became slaves to American Indians in the Great Northwest.

After a few months, the Indians arrived at a trading post named Fort Vancouver. There, the three men were released (likely sold or traded for more valuable goods) into the custody of Jean-Baptiste McLoughlin, who was with the Hudson Bay Company. McLoughlin smelled an opportunity to use the men to begin trading with Japan. He sent them to London in 1835 as a way of trying to convince the Crown to use them as a bargaining chip for opening up commerce. The Crown wasn't convinced, so they sent the three to Macau. Macau was a Portuguese port. The idea was to ship the three men back to Japan.

In Macau, the three men met Karl Friedrich August Gützlaff. Gützlaff was a Prussian Lutheran missionary. He had been born in northwestern Poland and had learned how to make saddles for horses. But his heart burned for God, and God had a plan to send him to Asia. Gützlaff became one of the first Protestant missionaries in Bangkok, Thailand, and Korea. By the time Otichi, Kyukichi, and Iwakichi reached Macau, Gützlaff was the first Lutheran missionary to China. Though Gützlaff was in China, he was also thinking about Japan. His problem? He had no one to help him learn Japanese. Gützlaff cut a deal with the three men. If they taught him colloquial Japanese by helping him translate the Gospel of John, his wife would teach them English. They agreed.

Otokichi became a Christ-follower in the process, and the earliest Japanese translation of Scriptures was brought to Japan.

God took sailors from *Japan* and a saddle-maker from *Poland*, and moved them through the United States, Europe, and Asia while also doing incredible work in them in the process. But the more prominent masterpiece is that God used the mess of storm, slavery, and being outcast to translate Scriptures so hundreds of thousands might hear about hope. God worked a masterpiece on a scale we can barely imagine.

Roman and Olya

One day when I was in the fourth grade, my whole world changed. It was the day I got glasses. My first pair were gold-rimmed and wire-framed. I remember staring out the window at how distinct the leaves in the trees were. Up until that point, my world had looked like a Van Gogh painting. I could make out shapes, forms, and colors, but details escaped me. I couldn't read signs or words unless they were ten inches from my face. The challenge with giving a fourth-grader wire-framed glasses is that he's sure, no matter how careful he is, to sit on them at some point. After the third time, my parents bought hard plastic glasses for me to match my thick plastic lenses.

There was a second change that happened right around my mid-forties. That was the day I received Lasik surgery. I was nervous. We walked into the clinic, and a tall, beautiful young woman met my wife and me with a smile and prepped me for the procedure. She had a slight accent, so I asked her where she was from. She said that she and her family had moved to the U.S. from Ukraine.

I had taken a short-term mission trip to Ukraine in 1995 and 1996. I had preached in the area of Izmail, a city that sits on the Danube. In the twenty years between those trips and the day of my procedure, I'd met dozens of Ukrainians, and not one of them had ever heard of it. Except for a map, it seemed as if I was the only one who knew about it! But on that day in 2015, I took another chance at connecting with someone over the city of Izmail. I told Olya that I had been there during those years. She asked me what I had done there, and I told her I had done some speaking. I then asked her how she came to Chicagoland, and she said her husband was attending Moody Bible School. That let me know she was likely a Christian. I told her that I had done some preaching. She asked me where, and I told her. It turns out that it was her home church! That evening, Olya called her mom and told her about the American who had come in for Lasik surgery who had preached in their church in Izmail. Her mom was able to recall one of the sermons I'd delivered there. The next morning was my check-up, and I brought a photo album in (without glasses!). In several of the photos I was seated directly across from her relatives. She knew all of the names and people.

We followed up with a dinner with Olya and her husband, Roman. Roman had felt God's call to ministry but needed experience in ministry and some mentoring. Soon after that, Roman and Olya came to serve at Grace Pointe, where Roman was one of our interns. Today, Roman is serving on pastoral staff in Florida.

Is it possible that God moved me to serve on a short-term trip to Ukraine so that one day I could connect with Roman and Olya? Was a part of his masterpiece to minister to the people in Ukraine at that time while also creating a connection that he'd weave back into my story twenty years later? Is it possible that God's power and plan are so great that he could reach across geography and time to connect Roman into pastoral ministry in Florida? Yes! That's how big God is.

Derek and Melissa

My freshman year of college was turbulent. I began as a Californian in Abilene, Texas. I drove three states to begin college, sight unseen. And though I enjoyed my time there, I couldn't justify it financially, so I returned home for my second semester of college. For that semester and only that semester, I attended Sierra College in Rocklin, California. For a few months, I made a terrible decision. I decided I would be all things to all people. At college, I would behave as if I didn't know Jesus, and at church, I would act as if I did. I was just tired of standing out from the crowd. I was sick of fighting the constant current around me and thought that perhaps I was missing something. Maybe the people who didn't know Jesus were blissfully happy . . . and didn't feel any guilt about sin. I, on the other hand, was aware of my sin. And I was tired of dealing with it. Maybe, I foolishly thought, the best way to deal with it was to be a situational Christian.

Melissa was born in Savannah, Georgia, but grew up in Washington State. She didn't grow up religious. Melissa had a love for musical theater and was uncertain about her future. By the time we met in California, she'd already signed up for the Army. One last musical, she thought. We met at a college production of *Fiddler on The Roof*. I was a musician, and she was an actress.

On our second date, Melissa told me we weren't going to kiss unless I told her why I was so different from all of the other guys she'd dated. My ears grew red (they do that when I get embarrassed or feel ashamed). I asked her what she meant. She told me that I had a peace and joy most guys she knew didn't have. I had to keep my hands from shaking as I explained to her that I belonged to Jesus. I told her I wasn't representing him very well. That night, we had a long conversation about faith. Melissa went back to her house and gave her life to Jesus. When she left my loft, I spent the next hour or two crying my heart out to God.

We dated throughout the spring. Melissa had turned twenty-one the previous January (before we met), and I became nineteen years old in June (after we met). Melissa was to deploy in July. Before she left for basic training, we had premarital sex. She left for basic training, and I (yet again) apologized to God. I was sick of myself and my sin. Soon after that, I signed up for a mission trip with YWAM on Mercy Ships. I was slated to leave that September.

In August, Melissa called me from basic training. I was working in a Christian bookstore, with her picture on my desk. She asked me to sit down. Having made it through basic training, she'd gotten a medical examination as a part of the exit process. The doctor told her she was pregnant with our son.

Melissa and I determined to marry. We were married a little over six months from the day we met. Privately, I thought the odds of us getting a divorce were high. We were young. We barely knew each other. We were in love, but love can fade. All I knew was that doing things my way had led me to that point. God needed to have the priority in our lives if we had any hope of success. I'd made a mess, and I needed a masterpiece. And God provided. We're coming up on nearly thirty years of blissful marriage, having traveled the world and followed him to places and people we love. We've seen a lot of panoramic views and we've discovered that God is a master artist.

The ending of the story of Joseph provides us a glimpse of the view from God's perspective. What we'll discover is breathtakingly beautiful, mysterious, loving, and hopeful. Like the best glimpses of what God is doing, it will leave us with a profound sense of how God uses messes for his masterpieces.

> After this, Joseph was told, "Behold, your father is ill." So, he took with him his two sons, Manasseh and Ephraim. And it was told to Jacob, "Your son Joseph has come to you." Then Israel summoned his strength and sat up in bed. And Jacob said to Joseph, "God Almighty appeared to me at Luz in the land of Canaan and blessed me, and said to me, 'Behold, I will make you fruitful and multiply you, and I will make of you a company of peoples and will give this land to your offspring after you for an everlasting possession.' And now your two sons, who were born to you in the land of Egypt before I came to you in Egypt, are mine; Ephraim and Manasseh shall be mine, as Reuben and Simeon are. And the children that you fathered after them shall be yours. They shall be called by the name of their brothers in their inheritance. (Gen. 48:1–6)

Something big was happening here. Look closely. First, God was bringing in the nations to his promises. He was redeeming those who appeared at first glance to be far away. He was turning outsiders into insiders. Second, God was moving them from bondage to freedom. Third, he was reminding us that his blood can cover a person and a nation, and be a means to save the world. God uses life to give life.

Outsiders to Insiders

Egypt was one of the most powerful empires in all of world history. The Israelites were few in number and seemingly insignificant. God decided to bring redemption into the world through the few. "It was not because you were more in number than any other people that the LORD set his love on you and chose you, for you were the fewest of all peoples" (Deut. 7:7). Pop quiz: If God wanted to reach the most powerful nations on earth with a knowledge of his presence and also bring the nations in as a part of his family, how would he do it if his starting point was one small family?

First, God put someone in a position to proclaim to the most powerful man on earth about his presence. In our story, Joseph declared God's presence and power to Pharaoh. In future stories, men like Daniel would announce the message of God to emperors of global dominance. Pharaoh knew Joseph wasn't an Egyptian, and yet he made him second in command of Egypt. The nations came to Egypt for food, where Joseph was in a position to proclaim the one true God to them too.

Joseph's wife was the daughter of a prominent priest. His father-in-law was polytheistic, as was all of Egypt. She, however, married a man who believed in Yahweh. Joseph's God became her God. Together they had children raised with Egyptian dress and culture, but who belonged to a family dedicated to Yahweh. Sound familiar? They were in the world, but they did not belong to the Egyptian world.

Joseph's sons, Ephraim and Manasseh, were born of mixed heritage. They were the product of a union between an Israelite herder and an upper-class Egyptian woman. They were half-Egyptian and half-Israelite. If bloodline were the standard for inclusion as people of God, they would have been appreciated but socially and spiritually excluded from the family tree of God's people. But God did something extraordinary and important.

Before Jacob (Israel) died he said, "Ephraim and Manasseh shall be mine, as Reuben and Simeon are" (Gen. 48:5). First, Israel adopted them as if they were among his own twelve sons, who would later become the twelve tribes of Israel. He went even further by bestowing a blessing on them. Scratch that. He bestowed THE blessing on them, a continuation of the blessing made from Abraham to Isaac to Jacob and now to Joseph's sons.

> The God before whom my fathers Abraham and Isaac walked, the God who has been my shepherd all my life long to this day, the angel who has redeemed me from all evil, bless the boys; and in them let my name be carried on, and the name of my fathers Abraham and Isaac; and let them grow into a multitude in the midst of the earth. (Gen. 48:15–16)

"Bless the boys." I love that. Ephraim and Manasseh became the representation of the tribe of Joseph. They became a part of God's family, and they were *half-Egyptian*. God was bringing the nations into his family.

Bondage to Freedom

Whenever we read the story of Joseph, we also see a progression of God's people into bondage. That bondage began slowly. First, Joseph was in bondage. Then he found freedom and redemption. Over time, after they settled in Goshen, the Israelites became slaves in Egypt, held in bondage. Later, by the leadership of Moses and the supernatural deliverance of God, they ran into freedom through the Red Sea. But then they chose bondage in the wilderness. They were held captive by their fear of the giants in the Promised Land. That fear killed off a generation until another generation chose the freedom God placed before them.

Bondage is easy to slip into. Sometimes, it comes violently and unexpectedly, as in the case of Joseph. One lousy act and someone finds themselves in jail, a loveless marriage, a bitter divorce, or a sudden career change. Sometimes it comes slowly over time. Circumstances change where we flourish, and little by little, freedom is removed until we find ourselves under the slavery of circumstances beyond our control. Sometimes the frog in the kettle boils gradually.

Sometimes, bondage is chosen. The daunting prospect of a courageous act causes us to be so gripped by fear that fear itself becomes the chain that weighs us down. The rope we first use as a lifeline may become a noose of terror.

In the story of Joseph, we saw bondage in all of its ugliness. But we also saw the potential for freedom. One poor decision can lead to a new future. The circumstances that try to kill us become the inspiration that sets us free. As with David, the fears we face mean the opportunity to wield a sling and a stone. We have the opportunity to see giants fall. What's the difference between bondage and freedom? Perspective. Victor Frankl, a concentration camp survivor, once wrote about how captivity isn't necessarily all-encompassing. It's how you choose to view what you're facing and who or what you decide to listen to. Bondage is nothing new. It's the status quo of the global system. But the dysfunction exists to tell us it doesn't need to be this way. Freedom is available in Jesus alone.

Many people say that they have a problem with the exclusivity of Jesus. In an Old Testament context, they would say that a view of a monotheistic God is a narrow view. Why serve one God when you can chase after many gods? But our problem isn't really with exclusivity.

I've yet to meet a person in love with *someone* who was angry that they were not in love with *everyone*. Loving a particular person is a part of the experience of love. We don't shake our fists at the sky, angry that we live under one sun. The exclusivity of the sun is what gives us the capacity for life. Whenever I have a headache and take an aspirin, I'm not angry at a system wherein every pill doesn't cure my headache. The medicine's exclusivity toward the problem is what makes it the right solution.

People don't have a problem with exclusivity. We have a problem with control. We don't want to give up control of our lives to God, because we like being in control. Instead, we submit to the gods we've created because it makes us god in the end. We'd rather provide myths and realities we've invented than give up our lives to a reality greater than ourselves. Some people actually prefer to live in the worlds of *Star Wars*, *Harry Potter*, or *Lord of the Rings*. But submitting to freedom we've created isn't freedom. It's a mirage of freedom.

There's a disorder known as "maladaptive daydreaming disorder." One person wrote, "People who suffer from maladaptive daydreaming can spend more than half their days in 'vivid alternative universes.'" When we create new realities, we're also in danger of losing touch with reality. True freedom only comes through the narrow doorway of giving up control to an exclusive God. But few choose the path to freedom because of its cost. The end of themselves is a high price to pay.

Ask any therapist, pastor, or counselor whether change comes when the person *says* they want to change but isn't desperate enough to change. Lip service is just lip service until the will is convinced that a better life demands to trust someone else's prescription or recommendation for new attitudes and actions. There is a saying: I'm willing to change when the pain of staying where I am exceeds the pain of change and the unknown.

Life for Life

I've walked you through some details to pay attention to. Let me point out one more because God uses everything in his masterpiece. There is no detail too small. You'll recall that Joseph's multi-colored robe was dipped in goat's blood. A goat was sacrificed so that the sons of Jacob could concoct a story about the death of their brother. This is a seemingly innocuous detail, isn't it? Why provide that level of specificity? It would be easy enough to say, "Then they took Joseph's robe and told Jacob their brother was dead." But the Bible is specific. It was the blood of a goat. Then, in Genesis 45:5, Joseph said, "God sent me here to preserve your life." The blood from a goat's death became the gateway for Joseph to be in a position for others to know life.

The Israelites settled in Goshen, and as time went on, a new Pharaoh came. The Egyptians grew resentful, and the Israelites were enslaved. When God was working miracles as signs of his power before the new Pharaoh, blood would be smeared on the doorposts of the Israelites so that death would pass over them. The blood was from a lamb. The lamb's death would be the gateway for the Israelites to know life. Goats and lambs were sacrificed so that others might know life.

In the New Testament, Jesus was in Jerusalem for Passover celebrations. There he was crucified for the sins of all. "He [Jesus] entered once for all into the holy places, not by means of the blood of goats and calves but by means of his own blood, thus securing an eternal redemption" (Heb. 9:12). His blood, not the blood of *goats*, became the conduit to life.

Life for life. God used the mess of the sons of Jacob to set up a masterpiece that would culminate with Jesus. Had Joseph not been an outcast, the Israelites would likely not have come into Egypt as a nation. Had they not been in Egypt, there would have been no need for a "pass over." Had there been no Exodus with its tremendous symbolism and power, the ultra-fickle religious crowd that gathered for Passover in Jerusalem would likely not have crucified Jesus. No crucifixion, no redemption for you and me. The detail of the goat's blood, an act that symbolized death, is a foreshadowing of how God can take death and use death as a conduit for life. What others use for evil, God uses for good. The cross, which was a symbol of death, became the place where we find the hope of life.

God can take immense suffering and turn it into something significant. Not a drop of blood is wasted in God's design. No tear is meaningless. You might be in pain, but God can use your pain for life. And that life can have a global and historical impact.

Alicia

One Tuesday, as I left the office for lunch, I received a message from a girl named Alicia. She wrote, "I'm so lost. Can we talk?" Alicia was in the ninth grade when I last saw her. I was on the periphery of her world in those days, and at least twenty years had gone by since then. We hadn't spoken in all that time. Yet she remembered me as someone to whom she could reach out. We soon set up a video chat.

Alicia explained to my wife and me that she was a divorced mom with a sixteen-year-old son. After telling us a little about her life over the last twenty years, she repeated what she had initially written. She said, "I'm so lost and I don't know what to do." I asked her if she had ever given control of her life to Jesus. She said no. That afternoon, Alicia gave control of her life to Jesus. Melissa shed tears of joy next to me as we prayed with her.

You never know how God will use your witness in the life of someone else. God decided that a little bit of contact in one season of life is what he would use years later to make an eternal difference in the life of someone else. In God's plan, no one is innocuous. Circumstances are repurposed. Pain has a process leading to healing and hope. He can use any of us in ways that bring beauty into this world.

Lessons from a New View

1. God longs to graft you into his family.

If you've ever seen any of the *National Lampoon Vacation* movies, you know about Cousin Eddie. There's an old saying, you can choose your friends, but you can't choose your family. Cousin Eddie is that family member with whom you might never normally associate. We all have times where we wish we could have chosen our family. Many children daydream about having been born into a family other than the family into which they were born. "Maybe," thinks a little boy or girl, "I come from a superhero family. Maybe I have superpowers no one else in this family has!"

In a stunning passage in the Bible, Jesus was asked to turn his attention from his spiritual family to his physical family, who were waiting just outside the door where he was teaching.

> And his mother and his brothers came and standing outside they sent to him and called him. And a crowd was sitting around him, and they said to him, "Your mother and your brothers are outside, seeking you." And he answered them, "Who are my mother and my brothers?" And looking about at those who sat around him, he said, "Here are my mother and my brothers! For whoever does the will of God, he is my brother and sister and mother." (Mk. 3:31–35)

God considers our spiritual family a priority!

God grafts us into his family when we join others who are owned by him. The phrase "Jesus is Lord" isn't just a confessional statement, it's a statement of family lineage and history. Consider the following Scriptures:

But to all who did receive him, who believed in his name, he gave the right to become children of God, who were born, not of blood nor of the will of the flesh nor of the will of man, but of God. (John 1:12–13)

See what kind of love the Father has given to us, that we should be called children of God; and so we are. The reason the world does not know us is that it did not know him. Beloved, we are God's children now, and what we will be has not yet appeared; but we know that when he appears, we shall be like him, because we shall see him as he is. (1 John 3:1–2)

So then you are no longer strangers and aliens, but you are fellow citizens with the saints and members of the household of God, built on the foundation of the apostles and prophets, Christ Jesus himself being the cornerstone, in whom the whole structure, being joined together, grows into a holy temple in the Lord. In him you also are being built together into a dwelling place for God by the spirit. (Eph. 2:19–22)

If I delay, you may know how one ought to behave in the household of God, which is the church of the living God, a pillar and buttress of the truth. (1 Tim. 3:15)

There are many differences between our physical and spiritual families, and nearly all of them are positive. Our spiritual family is different from our physical family in that there is a distinct clarity of purpose. We're commanded to love each other. When we give our lives to follow Jesus, we are told that a part of his leading and command is the intentional determination to love each other.

A new commandment I give to you, that you love one another: just as I have loved you, you also are to love one another. (John 13:34)

Beloved, let us love one another, for love is from God, and whoever loves has been born of God and knows God. Anyone who does not love does not know God, because God is love. In this the love of God was made manifest among us, that God sent his only Son into the world, so that we might live through him. (1 John 4:7–9)

I bristle at Christians who believe their primary role is to criticize the church. Of course, those who criticize say they do it in love, but it's hard to tell from their tone. Most of the time, it comes across as "I'm so smart that only I can see how the church is so wrong." Famous Christian bloggers, authors, and teachers have made entire careers on pointing out everything the church isn't rather than what it is. They tend to work from theory, comparing it to what is perfect. In reality, they speak from a mess to a mess.

Let's be clear. The church is far from perfect. The church has many flaws and errors, and we shouldn't avoid speaking the truth. We should warn and teach the truth. But a deep love for the people of God should shine through each critique.

I've met some mean and petty people who call themselves Christians. Let's set aside for a moment whether or not they are Christians, and assume they are. Ugly behavior is wrong. And let's also be honest to say there are mean non-Christians. There are mean and petty people everywhere.

When I was a boy, we lived for two years in Los Lunas, New Mexico. My father pastored a small church there. We were poor but happy. We had milk because one of our church members had cattle and offered us milk for free. Most of our clothes were either handmade or hand-me-downs. One year, Dad decided he would give me a birthday gift by buying me a bicycle. Dad obtained a second job on the night shift at a local Circle K (something like a 7-Eleven) and managed to save enough to purchase me the gift. It was an inexpensive white, ten-speed bicycle. I'll never forget how humbled and overjoyed I was to receive it. The bicycle cost less than $100, but for our family, it was a significant sacrifice. And I was aware of the significance of the gift and its cost.

A family in the church learned Dad had given me a bicycle and promptly left the church. Some people leave churches like turtles (slow and quiet) while others leave like skunks (loud and stinky). This family left like a skunk. The reason? In their view, no pastor should be able to afford gifting their son a bicycle. The irony was that this same family was wealthy!

I grew up experiencing the good, the bad, and the ugly of church life. If you're looking for perfect people, the church is the wrong place to look. Imperfection is everywhere. Criticism of flaws takes virtually no effort.

Imperfect as they were, the family of Israel was God's chosen family. You might believe it's irrelevant that Joseph's half-Egyptian sons became Israel's sons. But it's profound. Because your becoming an integral part of a church body (which God grafted you into) is a difference maker to your continued journey of health and wholeness. Here are five reasons why church is a difference maker for you:

Difference Maker #1: Mutual Submission

When dysfunction and conflict arise in the church, the spiritual family has learned to humble itself before God. We realize that sin is something we have to suspect in ourselves first. The spiritual family doesn't begin by assuming we're in a competition for proving who is best. Instead, we're all humbled by the realization that we don't deserve God's grace. We feel privileged to be in his family. Countless conflicts are addressed between Christians in the local church when forgiveness is sought. Conflict swiftly leads to a resolution based on mutual submission to Jesus as Lord. In a physical family, there is no joint submission to an authority higher than every member of the family. But in a spiritual family, there's mutual submission, and therefore, a shared basis for resolution.

This is no small thing. Counselors and therapists work hard to get two parties to admit their shortcomings. It takes a monumental effort to swallow pride. But a resolution is more accessible when both parties put their pride to the side to find a resolution. As a pastor, I find this is one of the most challenging parts of helping others. What typically happens is that both parties begin by admitting they aren't perfect, and then find ways to explain why they are better than the other person. Pride, of course, comes before a fall. Pride is what leads us to the path of feeling entitled, demanding, or manipulative of someone else. The church is full of dysfunctional people. But the church has the benefit of calling on mutual submission, which it already learned because submission was the requirement to enter into God's family. We all died to self to live for Christ. In Scripture, Paul called himself "the chief of sinners." He wasn't trying to "out-humble" the next guy. Paul wasn't making this a point of pride. Instead, he was reflecting a specific posture. It is the posture of the local church, which is a very different posture from that of the world. Every failure of church leadership or scandal within the church begins first with pride. Humility is what drives health. The spiritual family starts with a posture bent toward health.

Difference Maker #2: Selfless Love

Our love for God drives our love for one another. In fact, when we don't like each other but are seeking to be obedient to Jesus, we choose love because Jesus gave us no other choice! In the physical family, love can't be forced, but it can be fostered. While love can't be coerced in the spiritual family, there's an appeal to obedience. We can choose to obey Jesus even when we don't feel like loving. Not only is love fostered, but also it becomes a consequence of individual obedience to Jesus. As we love him, we come together in our love one for another. To dig deeper into this idea, we should ask what Howard Jones asked when he sang, "*What is love anyway?*"

If we measure love purely by how we feel, we're in trouble. But that's not to say that feeling has no value. If I look at my wife and never feel love for her, there's something wrong. But if my love for my wife is dictated by my feelings for her, that is equally wrong. Some days, I wake up and say, "Oh! It's you" with a feeling of bliss. Other days, I wake up and say, "Oh! It's you" with a feeling of indifference. If love were based on feelings, then I'm in and out of love all the time. The Bible teaches that at its core, love isn't a feeling, but a posture of selflessness:

By this we know love, that he laid down his life for us, and we ought to lay down our lives for the brothers. (1 John 3:16)

Beloved, let us love one another, for love is from God, and whoever loves has been born of God and knows God. Anyone who does not love does not know God, because God is love. In this the love of God was made manifest among us, that God sent his only Son into the world, so that we might live through him. In this is love, not that we have loved God but that he loved us and sent his Son to be the propitiation for our sins. Beloved, if God so loved us, we also ought to love one another. No one has ever seen God; if we love one another, God abides in us and his love is perfected in us. (1 John 4:7–12)

For God so loved the world, that he gave his only Son, that whoever believes in him should not perish but have eternal life. (John 3:16)

Scriptural love is specific. It's associated with romance but isn't confused with romance. Love begins not centripetally, but centrifugally. Love is generous. Love expands and includes. Love moves out, away from you to invest in others. In church our love for God translates and challenges us relationally with each other. Our commitment to love each other is a testimony for others to know of our belonging to God. In other words, when someone is being mean in the world, everyone may call them a "jerk" but can't do much about it. When someone is a jerk in church, we can appeal to them in humility, and love them not because they deserve love, but because we are conduits of God's love to others. And we can remind them that they are conduits as well.

Right now, the church is divided by politics. But we are to be united in our love for Jesus and one another. We are to love our spiritual family. That's a biblical command. Fellow Christ-followers are not enemies. If you think they are, then start loving your enemies.

Difference Maker #3:
Common Vision—Unity in Diversity

In the world around us, there are many noble causes. People champion some beautiful things: promoting human rights, fighting against poverty, ending human trafficking, promoting freedom, stopping racism or exploitation, promoting fairness, and so on. Why does the human race need to find things to champion? We'll create meaning out of the meaningless to experience a shared common vision. For example, each year American football teams go crazy. Football players will endure permanent damage to their bodies for the hope of having a ring that indicates they won a Super Bowl game. Football is a game that is meaningless in its merit. But we've infused incredible meaning to it. The game serves no higher purpose other than to have fun (which many parents seem to forget as they cheer on the Pee Wee football game at their local field). We've created entire industries that exist for the pursuit of a shared vision of meaninglessness (video games, anyone?). We're all searching for the ties that bind us together.

The church of God is powerful because it shares a common vision for an experienced new reality described as the "kingdom of God." It's the opposite of creating meaning from the meaningless. It's seeking to express meaning out of the deeply meaningful. We're trying to find the words to communicate a reality that is deep and unseen. If anything, the church struggles with turning the meaningful into the meaningless! Our sin tends to reduce the truth to the trite. Now, which side of the "common vision" coin would you prefer to be on?

Difference Maker #4: Diversity in Unity

There are two famous "12" chapters in the Bible: Romans 12 and 1 Corinthians 12. Both confront the subject of unity and diversity. Rather than go through both, let me provide Paul's summation in Romans 12:4–5, "For as in one body we have many members, and the members do not all have the same function, so we, though many, are one body in Christ, and individually members one of another."

One great fear that many have in becoming followers of Christ, and therefore a part of a local church, is that their uniqueness will be drained away. We begin to believe the lie that all Christians look and behave either like spiritual nerds or wannabes. They think that to be a Christian means to wear white patent leather shoes, listen 24/7 to Bill and Gloria Gaither, and wear clothes that went out of fashion years ago. "Mom jeans," anyone? The other stereotype is that Christians are so busy being aspirational and inspirational models that they speak in spiritual euphemisms. They start wearing clothes that scream, "Aren't I just the coolest?" They've never heard a U2 song that couldn't be turned into a spiritual principle. They're like hipsters, except that people want to be like them. (Quick joke: How many hipsters does it take to screw in a lightbulb? Answer: You wouldn't know, it's kind of an obscure number.)

But the truth is far less stereotypical. In reality, the church is full of people derived from all ethnicities, backgrounds, and socio-economic strata. And each one of them was created individually by God to make a unique contribution. 1 Corinthians 12:24b–25 says, "But God has so composed the body, giving greater honor to the part that lacked it, that there may be no division in the body, but that the members may have the same care for one another." Essentially, Paul is saying that no one person is held in higher value than another person because we all need each other uniquely. As the church grows, so too does its diversity and unity.

Along with diversity comes frustration because we tend to like people who are like us. But we need people who aren't like us. Thankfully, we don't always have to choose between the two. A part of following God is trusting that he provides for our needs. The people in the local church, with their flaws and frustrations, may be just what we need to provide the stimulus and friction that God uses to work us into his unique design. I mentioned sports earlier. One great value of team sports is this principle. Your quarterback shouldn't function like your offensive lineman. But both are needed to play a great football game.

There's another point regarding diversity: not only are we diversely gifted, but the church is also diverse in its process toward spiritual maturity. We tend to think of church as being either in or out. And there's some truth to that because belonging to the kingdom of God is a binary proposition. Jesus is Lord or he isn't Lord. But while there is a point of demarcation, there is a lot of process in the journey. There's a journey to the Cross, a process of laying ourselves down so that God can reign. There's a process toward spiritual maturity. Some people in the church will be immature in Christ.

The road toward spiritual maturity can be frustrating. We have to learn how to move from the "rollercoaster of love" to a deep, committed kind of love. We gain knowledge but can't dip over into legalism. We learn how grace isn't passive, but active; it moves through us to others, and this activates mutual accountability. We work through surrendering major character struggles in our lives. Even the spiritually mature, though rooted and devoted to God, struggle with comfort versus sacrifice. The church is full of people who are diverse and different in the spiritual maturity process.

I think this is often forgotten by many of the critics of the church. The assumption is that the church isn't messy. But the church is also full of people who are in process. Holiness is doing its work in our lives, but to do so our lives have to be "heated up" like ore in a refinery. The ugly stuff rises to the surface—our attitudes, actions, responses, comments, tempers, and so on. And then God scrapes off the dross so that over time, the treasures we are start to shine. On the surface, the church may appear like any other nonprofit organization. But beneath the surface, there's a process of refinement that is unlike anything the world has ever seen.

People tend to be at their crankiest when they're sick or suffering. I've rarely gotten the flu and thought, "Let me think about how loving I can be right now." Instead, I'm thinking about Vicks VapoRub, a dark room, and a lot of sleep. When I'm miserable, I don't want to respond in love. Similarly, when circumstances in our lives cause us discomfort, our old self emerges. We can be cranky. We can also become clueless. Like Joseph, we wear multi-colored coats and wonder why we're getting the reaction we do from our spiritual family. The church is full of clueless people God is cluing in. It's full of sick people God is bringing to health. God's church is diverse in many ways, but that's a part of its beauty. God is building his church. He's teaching us to see one another through the lens of character change.

Difference Maker #5: Mutual Encouragement

Steven is an older missionary I knew while living overseas. Steven is an encourager. He's someone you want to be around because he recognizes what God is doing in you. And that results in your feeling better about the person you're becoming. There were some days I wanted to throw in the towel on ministry. God seemed to know the right time to connect me with Steven.

Lonnie is a spiritual hero of mine. He continues to be an encouragement to me because he didn't just say, "Go for it!" Instead, he said, "Let's talk about who God is and who we are. How courageous can we be to be as much like him as possible? What do we have to change or embrace?" Every time I had a conversation with Lonnie, my ministry battery would get charged up. I started thinking and dreaming in new ways.

Bill is a mentor God sent my way at the right time (*kairos*) in my life. He believed in me so much that he risked his relationship network by connecting me with people he knew. Bill was always thinking about the next best way to advance the kingdom of God. Nothing has ever seemed to slow him down, including age, circumstance, or family situation. Bill is an encourager.

Early in the COVID-19 pandemic, I was outside working on my yard when a parade of a hundred cars began to honk and holler in our neighborhood. One by one, they slowly rolled by my house with signs of appreciation and encouragement for me. As tears welled up in my eyes, I thanked God for the thoughtfulness and support of God's church.

I could go on and on telling stories of countless men and women who took the time to say a kind word, to commit to pray with me or my family, who rolled up their sleeves and said, "Let's get to work!" I'm surrounded by incredible people. I'm a part of God's family.

As God's spiritual family, we learn to work together, building each other up instead of tearing each other down. That building up should inspire us to encourage others. I know so many who receive encouragement and then wait for more encouragement. They can't seem to get enough! But in Scripture, we're encouraged to encourage others. Encouragement is reciprocal. We want everyone in God's spiritual family to be the version of themselves God created them to become. We want to participate with the Holy Spirit through encouragement to be like Jesus! We teach encouragingly. We even warn as encouragement. "Therefore encourage one another and build one another up" (1 Thess. 5:11).

The story of Joseph reads like a great story of individual accomplishment. We saw Joseph alone in a cistern. We saw him as a lone Israelite in Egypt. But look closer. A caravan of people picked up Joseph. Joseph had great relationships with the other workers in Potiphar's house. When Joseph went to prison, he listened and encouraged others. Joseph was a voice of encouragement to the cupbearer. Joseph was an encouragement to Pharaoh that God had a purpose for Pharaoh's dream! God provided Joseph with a beautiful Egyptian wife and two amazing sons. And then, just when you think it couldn't get any better, God re-introduced Joseph to his spiritual (and also physical) family. It was a family in whom God had also been at work.

An imperfect family? Yes. But the story of Joseph's life is one that still ended in community. An entire nation was re-located in the best Egypt had to offer. Joseph was to have more spiritual brothers and sisters than he could have ever anticipated. Joseph's world opened up as God worked through him in the context of relationships.

> So if there is any encouragement in Christ, any comfort from love, any participation in the spirit, any affection and sympathy, complete my joy by being of the same mind, having the same love, being in full accord and of one mind. Do nothing from selfish ambition or conceit, but in humility count others more significant than yourselves. Let each of you look not only to his own interests, but also to the interests of others. Have this mind among yourselves, which is yours in Christ Jesus. (Phil. 2:1–5a)

2. Remember your birthright.

As we come to a new view with our new self, we must remember to whom we belong. Joseph never forgot he was an Israelite, even though by the end of his life, he spoke, dressed, walked, and talked like an Egyptian.

Though Joseph was rejected by his family, he never forgot his family. He continued to long for his father, Jacob, and his brother Benjamin. He remembered the family to whom he belonged. "For in Christ Jesus you are all sons of God, through faith" (Gal. 3:26).

You are a child of God with great things waiting for you as an inheritance. You have a birthright! Behave like a son or daughter of God. Represent his family. Begin identifying areas in your life where you behave as if you aren't worth that birthright and let them go. Embrace the attitudes and actions of the redeemed.

God wants you not to behave as if you are defeated, but as if you live in victory. This is not an arrogant kind of behavior (based on "I deserve"), because you didn't do anything to earn that birthright. The birthright speaks to your value and your belonging to God. Your behavior should reflect the knowledge that whatever circumstance you may find yourself in, God has not abandoned you. When depression calls out your name and tells you that you are worthless, God reminds you that you are of imminent worth. When you believe the lie that you are beyond forgiveness, or when you think you can forgive yourself, don't believe those lies! You can't forgive you. You are a child of a God who specializes in miracle repairs. God forgives. Remember your birthright. You have a future. You have hope, and your life matters.

When I was a junior in high school, a friend of mine came to the place I was working and spoke briefly with my manager. The manager found me in the back of the store and told me in a somber tone that I had a friend who needed to speak with me, and that I had the rest of the day off. Confused, I went out to the food court. There I was told that a mutual friend of ours had died by suicide.

Traci was in our church college group. She'd heard about Jesus, attended church regularly, and sung worship songs with gusto. But she also sought her validation from men. Once she felt no man wanted her, so too her desire to live waned. She hanged herself at a Suicide Prevention Facility. Traci had forgotten that her value lay in her birthright. When you forget Who it is to whom you belong, this can open the door to all kinds of destruction. Chaos enters in. Lives are broken and destroyed.

Sometimes the most proactive thing you can do is to remind yourself over and over again that you are worthwhile. Brennan Manning once wrote, "My trust in God flows out of the experience of his loving me, day in and day out, whether the day is stormy or fair, whether I'm sick or in good health, whether I'm in a state of grace or disgrace. He comes to me where I live and loves me as I am." The God of the Universe knows your name and cares for you. You are of immense value to him because you are his child! Because of your birthright, you have access to him.

> Ask, and it will be given to you; seek, and you will find; knock, and it will be opened to you. For everyone who asks receives, and the one who seeks finds, and to the one who knocks it will be opened. Or which one of you, if his son asks him for bread, will give him a stone? Or if he asks for a fish, will give him a serpent? If you then, who are evil, know how to give good gifts to your children, how much more will your Father who is in heaven give good things to those who ask him! (Matt. 7:7–11)

3. Build on humility and discernment as your foundation for courage.

If you're looking from a mountaintop and you don't feel small, then your mountain isn't high or big enough. A new view leads us to a sense of humility. Humility can fuel courage. Humility has become anachronistic at this point in history. The reward for bragging is fame. Everyone seems to be chasing fame. President Trump (whatever you think of him) is not known for his humility. LeBron James calls himself the greatest player of all time (and he's still playing basketball)! It strains the imagination nowadays to think of someone prominent who is confident, but humble.

Humility has not always been such an anathema. Albert Einstein said, "A true genius admits that he/she knows nothing." Even William Shakespeare wrote, "The fool doth think he is wise, but the wise man knows himself to be a fool." Having humility does not mean you view yourself with less value. Rick Warren wrote, "True humility is not thinking less of yourself; it is thinking of yourself less." It merely means you have a perspective that doesn't assume an arrogant posture. You are humbled because you know enough to know what you don't know! Every person with a PhD should have humility! Instead, we often buy into our press. We enjoy being the center of attention and start believing that we deserve recognition. Again, that idea of "deserve" is at the root of a lot of bad attitudes.

C. S. Lewis wrote, "As long as you are proud you cannot know God. A proud man is always looking down on things and people: and, of course, as long as you are looking down you cannot see something that is above you." Abraham Lincoln said, "I have been driven many times upon my knees by the overwhelming conviction that I had nowhere else to go. My own wisdom and that of all about me seemed insufficient for that day." Building on humility will give you a perspective that will limit dysfunction by putting boundaries on the "self" in your centeredness.

It's a shame we tend to unbundle the two words "humility" and "discernment." In reality, humility does not detract from discernment. They go together.

APPLICATION

1. As you look back on your life and you see the life transitions God has brought you through, how have those transitions set up the future God had (or has yet) in store for you?

2. We sometimes miss the beauty of God's plan for the nations because we are too focused on us. Read Romans 10:9–18. What do you notice here about how God saves, who he saves, and how his message is proclaimed to the nations?

3. How did you hear about the Good News of Jesus? Which relational lines did God use to graft you into his family? Who is God calling you to reach out to, to bear witness to his Good News relationally?

4. In Matthew 12:46–50 Jesus emphasized spiritual family, and in Luke 9:57–62 he again placed the physical family in the context of following himself. How do these passages impact our focus within our church relationships?

5. Members of Joseph's family went through significant character changes—some intentionally and some by circumstances. All had to have the desire both (1) to change, and (2) to exercise different responses as each new situation presented itself. In what ways do you think the church allows others to grow and mature in Christ? How have you seen impatience in yourself?

12:
More Ahead

"Since we are all prone to live selfishly, it is necessary that there should be something within us to offset this tendency." —Helen Keller

■

"Not only that, but we rejoice in our sufferings, knowing that suffering produces endurance, and endurance produces character, and character produces hope, and hope does not put us to shame, because God's love has been poured into our hearts through the Holy Spirit who has been given to us." —Romans 5:3–5

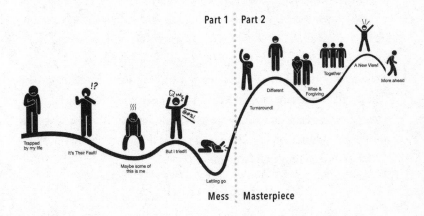

Psalm 37:4 reads, "Delight yourself in the LORD, and he will give you the desires of your heart." As we end our journey together, and with the knowledge that your journey will continue, let's ask a basic question: "Did God give Joseph the desires of his heart?" In other words, was God true to his Word?

What was the desire of Joseph's heart? What lay at the heart of his dysfunctional response to a broken world?

At the end of his life, did others recognize his significance? By any measure, the answer is a resounding YES. God gave Joseph the desires of Joseph's heart. But he did not give that desire through the person Joseph was. God chose to give it through the person Joseph could be. This distinction matters. To receive all your heart's desires before your character has the capacity to handle them can be more damaging than helpful.

Hinds Feet on High Places is a book describing how hard paths can lead to great heights. In it, Much Afraid (the main character) travels with her companions, Sorrow and Suffering, to develop spiritual maturity and discover freedom by the Good Shepherd. It's about character growth. It's about the mess of the valleys, the masterpieces of the mountains, and the steps in between. By the end of the book, Much Afraid's name is changed to Grace and Glory. Sorrow and Suffering become Joy and Peace. We see this journey reflected in the life of Joseph as well.

God's intention for you is good. God allows circumstances into your life for your good. He's not out to get you. He's not finding ways to torture you.

Some stories end in a "happily ever after." But life is rarely like that. That doesn't mean life can't end well. But it does mean that life is rarely a fairy tale ending. The end of Joseph's story appears to close with the words "Happily ever after." But it's not long before buried insecurities surface. We're not done with Joseph's story yet.

Joseph: More Ahead

When Israel died, Joseph wept over his father's corpse. Israel was embalmed in the Egyptian tradition. The embalming process took forty days. The Egyptians then took another seventy days of mourning. Israel's death was noted by Pharaoh, whom Jacob himself had blessed earlier in the story.

The family took Israel's embalmed corpse (in the Egyptian style and tradition) to Canaan. They buried him in the family cave there and lamented his death for seven days, one-tenth the amount of time the Egyptians mourned over Jacob. The residents of Canaan mistook the lamenting and mourning of Jacob's family for Egyptians grieving for the loss of an Egyptian. It's a stunning description of a family that has now adopted the culture and style of their host country. It's a great reminder that though we may appear to belong in one place, we belong to another. Jacob's family was not home yet. Neither are we.

Sometimes our old insecurities get the better of us. Joseph's brothers wondered what Joseph would do now that their father was dead. Would Joseph exact revenge now that he had no father to consider? Was Joseph just biding his time until Israel died? They said, "It may be that Joseph will hate us and pay us back for all the evil that we did to him" (Gen. 50:15). The old insecurities resurfaced. The brothers hatched a scheme, just as they had done in the old times.

They couldn't throw Joseph into a well this time. What they could do is tell Joseph something their father said that Joseph could not substantiate. They told Joseph that Israel gave a command for Joseph before he died. This command was a serious, sacred thing to say because it carried the weight of the family patriarch. What did the brothers of Joseph say their father commanded? "Forgive your brothers" (Gen. 50:17). How very convenient for them.

Scripture records, "Joseph wept when they spoke to him" (Gen. 50:17). Maybe he wept because he knew they were lying. Perhaps Joseph wept because, in countless conversations with Jacob, his father had never mentioned it. Perhaps he wept because they assumed the worst of him when all he'd demonstrated to them was the best. It's so hard when people think the worst of you. That's like a punch in the gut.

Years ago, I had people I thought were friends who assumed the worst of a letter I'd written. I didn't write the letter with the intent they interpreted. But instead of giving me the benefit of the doubt, they assumed the worst of me. They were just waiting for an excuse to consider me the person they projected onto me. That hurt.

Joseph wept. His brothers went a step further. They bowed down before him and told him they were his servants. As the reader, I was so frustrated by this that I found myself silently urging Joseph to kick them while they were bowing down. Here we go again!

But Joseph didn't do that. Joseph kept his focus on God. "Joseph said to them, 'Do not fear, for am I in the place of God? As for you, you meant evil against me, but God meant it for good, to bring it about that many people should be kept alive, as they are today. So do not fear; I will provide for you and your little ones.' Thus, he comforted them and spoke kindly to them" (Gen. 50:19–21).

Joseph reminded his brothers, who shouldn't have needed reminding, of the goodness of God. He essentially repeated the same sentiment from earlier in the story when they were afraid after he revealed himself as their brother. But he added some assurance.

Joseph once again put aside his ego and hurt. Once more, it was up to him to be the gracious one. He chose humility when he could have chosen to be indignant. And not only did he bear the responsibility to keep them in the right perspective, but he also took the initiative to comfort and speak kindly to them. Let's not pretend that's always easy. Sometimes, it's just exhausting. It's tiring to be the one person who seems to be protecting a new way of relating. Why does it seem as if it's always up to us?

As a father, I've often found myself in the position of protecting a family practice, not because it was popular, but because it was right for the family. There were loads of eye-rolls at having to eat dinner at the dinner table instead of eating scattered throughout the house. Attending church gatherings was sometimes done by dragging my kids into the car. They wanted a choice, but I knew that the decision was not to their benefit. There's a riptide in life that pulls you away from God. All it takes is to stop swimming, to cease trying to follow him intentionally. Someone has to love others enough to encourage them to swim when everyone else seems unmotivated to work. That's the kind and loving thing to do, but it's also exhausting and sometimes lonely. That's the position of Joseph. Have we ended Joseph's story where we began? No. Even though this is yet another episode in the family story of dysfunction and mess, dysfunction no longer *defines* the family.

Joseph died in Egypt. He lived to be very old. He knew his great-grandchildren, who loved him. And Joseph treated them with as much love and kindness as he treated his sons. Before Joseph died, he promised his brothers that God would eventually lead his people back to the Promised Land. Joseph knew that God's promises were sure. Times were good, but they were about to get hard. Joseph did not live to see the hard times of the Israelites in Egypt. What a gift!

Joseph was embalmed and put in a coffin in Egypt. But his bones would go with the people of God. The family that once sold him to a caravan to Egypt would be the same family who would carry him out of Egypt. His bones would belong to the people and the places of God. Joseph would not be forgotten again or left behind. Not even in death.

More Hope Ahead

God's heart is one of selfless love. God loves you. His love isn't the kind that uses and discards you. His love is the kind that is generous, thoughtful, and immensely faithful. Lamentations 3:22–23 says, "The steadfast love of the LORD never ceases; his mercies never come to an end; they are new every morning; great is your faithfulness."

Wait, what book was that in again? Lamentations. What's a "lamentation"? Merriam-Webster defines it as "an expression of sorrow, mourning, or regret." In the middle of a book on the difficulty of life, Lamentations reminds us the steadfast love of God and his never-ending mercies begin anew with each new day! We can rely on his faithfulness.

Once we understand that we can't always control our circumstances, but that we can count on a God who desires his best for us and that his heart is full of love for us, we can start to let go of that which we can't control and embrace that which is promised. Our frustration is no longer an endless cycle based on anxiety or fear, because worry is replaced with trust and fear with love.

Joseph's story is a story of hope despite the appearance of hopelessness. Hope was a companion. God taught Joseph how to hope without trying to dictate outcomes. In the process, Joseph became a conduit of hope for the hopeless.

God wants us to live our lives on the side of hopefulness. "May the God of hope fill you with all joy and peace in believing, so that by the power of the Holy Spirit you may abound in hope" (Rom. 15:13). God wants us his people to be hopeful. Our hope is to rest in God's abilities and not our own. "Why are you cast down, O my soul, and why are you in turmoil within me? Hope in God; for I shall again praise him, my salvation and my God" (Ps. 42:5–6a).

When William Borden was young, he wanted to be a missionary. But circumstances kept getting in the way. His father died, and he took over his father's successful business. Finally, after many years of longing and faithfulness to his familial duty, Borden left to go to China. En route, he contracted cerebral meningitis in Cairo, Egypt, and died.

In our view of things, the end of his life was one of potential unfulfilled. Or was it? When William Borden died, letters were published from all over the world by people who said his faithfulness to Jesus radically changed their trajectories. God kept Borden in the US to inspire, teach, and encourage. Borden taught Sunday School and started various ministries, all while longing to be a missionary. And while it may have seemed cruel that life did not take him immediately to China, God was using Borden's life to change people. Borden inspired people when he left the family business. He encouraged people when he was training to be a missionary. And he inspired people along the way. His was an ordinary life with extraordinary purpose. On his gravestone is this inscription, "Apart from faith in Christ, there is no explanation of such a life."

Jim and Elizabeth Elliot left as missionaries to South America. Jim was killed after weeks and months of planning and preparing to meet with an indigenous group of people who were suspicious of outsiders. Others might see his short life and think, "What a waste!" And yet, God used Jim's death to inspire a renewed commitment to share the gospel with that tribe. The tribe later embraced that missionary team, and many would experience the radical transformation of the gospel. Jim's death led his wife, Elizabeth, to write a book that would inspire thousands of men and women to serve Christ wholeheartedly as missionaries. God even used Jim Elliot's journals as an inspiration for young men seeking God's will. I know because I am one of those young men inspired by his life.

You might feel as if people will forget your life of faithfulness. But God has a way of making sure you aren't forgotten. When God redeems, he redeems completely. Your legacy and reputation may be beyond your control, but they are not beyond his control. The same family that put you in a mess may be the same family that brings you out of it.

Moses took Joseph's bones out of Egypt when the Israelites escaped the clutches of an evil empire. God allowed an entire generation to die in the wilderness, but Joseph's bones weren't buried in the wilderness. When Joshua led God's people into the Promised Land, Joshua buried Joseph's bones there. Joseph was never forgotten. Generations would recognize Joseph's significance. Your life and legacy can have a lasting impact.

You may have dreams of significance. You may be stuck in difficult relational dynamics. Or others may have put you in a pit, and you're finding your life careening out of control. The pit you're in can be a part of his purpose if you'll trust, obey, and believe him along the way. There's a bigger story at work. God will lead you to a more comprehensive significance than you can imagine because God can turn your mess into his masterpiece. That's the story of Joseph. It can also be your story.

For we are God's masterpiece. He has created us anew in Christ Jesus, so we can do the good things he planned for us long ago. (Eph. 2:10, NLT)

APPLICATION

1. As you look back on your life, what are the spiritual milestones where you caught a glimpse of how God is using your life for a purpose bigger than you?

2. Which peoples or nations should you learn to love as God loves? In which ways can you grow a heart for others so that you would view them as your own family?

3. To be a follower of Jesus is to go against the flow of humanity. In many ways, that can be a difficult challenge and one in which we can feel alone in the effort. We see sinful systems and decisions that hurt rather than heal. What people do you know of who stood out so entire family trajectories, systems of sin (racism, poverty, slavery, conflict, etc.), or nations could see the mighty hand of God at work? What do they have in common?

4. Write down the most difficult moments of your spiritual journey, the places or seasons where you questioned God and his future for you, or the moments that left you most confused. What did those moments reveal about your character in Christ and your journey toward spiritual maturity?

5. People are not always what they seem. What about that is tragic? How do you and I behave in the same way?

ACKNOWLEDGMENTS

I'm deeply indebted to so many who have been patient and kind throughout this process. Thank you, Nancy Clausen, for hearing content you believed would make a great book. Thank you for guiding me through the initial stages of development. Without you, I would not have written this.

Thank you, Christine Weaver-Crafton, David Webster, Daniel Weaver, Lori Pritchard, Traci Johnson, and so many others who read either entire early drafts or portions, offering feedback. My sister, in particular, spent hours reading and offering suggestions for making the manuscript presentable.

Thank you to Jon Sweeney, editor extraordinaire at Paraclete Publishing. I appreciate your encouragement and direction to cull the best out of the process. To the whole team, Robert Edmonson, Michelle Rich, Rachel McKendree, and so many more at Paraclete, I'm deeply honored to be a part of this process. A book truly takes a village.

Thank you to my wife, Melissa, for the hours I was home but not present. When my occupied mind took me out of the building, you never once complained. I love you.

To my own family—alive and deceased—I'm astonished by the grace of God in allowing me to be a part of you. My prayer is that faithfulness will be the marker of our tribe as we seek to be God's people following his leadership to others.

To my spiritual family of God's local church: may we be the points of grace in the places we live, work, and play. May others know we belong to our Lord by our love one for another. You inspire and encourage me. "Him we proclaim, warning everyone and teaching everyone with all wisdom, that we may present everyone mature in Christ" (Col. 1:28).

ABOUT THE AUTHOR

Derek Webster is an author, teacher, and the lead pastor at Grace Pointe church, a multi-campus church based in Naperville, Illinois. With nearly thirty years in full-time ministry, Derek and his family have planted several churches internationally and Derek has coached hundreds more on cultural engagement, church planting, and change management. His first book, *Unlocking the Soul of a City*, brought much of this expertise to bear by helping leaders know and reach cities globally. Today, along with pastoring Grace Pointe and completing his PhD at Trinity Evangelical Divinity School, Derek continues to teach, speak, and consult globally on leadership, culture, and mission. He and his wife have raised three boys and are the proud grandparents of two grandchildren.

Photo by Amy Dutton

LINKS AND NOTES

Introduction

x   *a gun to launch four-pound dead chickens:* Jon Excell, "June 1944: The chicken cannon," *The Engineer*, May 19, 2008. https://www. theengineer.co.uk/this-week-in-1944-the-chicken-cannon/.

Chapter One

4   *the governor called for a statewide house quarantine:* J. B. Pritzker, "Executive Order 2020-11," Mar. 23, 2020. https://www2.illinois. gov/Pages/Executive-Orders/ExecutiveOrder2020-11.aspx

9   *Character cannot be developed in ease and quiet:* Helen Keller, *The Open Door* (Garden City, NY: Doubleday, 1957), 15.

Chapter Two

15n1   *It wasn't me:* Shaggy feat. Rikrok. 2000. "It Wasn't Me," track 10 on *Hot Shot*, MCA-Geffen.

15n2   *I talked a few weeks ago with a lady:* Lee Strobel, *The Case for Faith* (Grand Rapids, MI: Zondervan, 2000), 231.

22n1   *WOO stands for "winning others over":* Tom Rath, *Strengthsfinder 2.0* (New York: Gallup Press, 2007), 169.

22n2   *Dysfunction ignored is a broken merry-go-round:* Kacey Musgraves, "Merry Go 'Round," track 3 on *Same Trailer, Different Park*, Mercy Nashville.

24n1   *Self-efficacy refers to an individual's belief:* APA Dictionary of Psychology. "Self-efficacy." American Psychological Association, 2020. https://dictionary.apa.org/self-efficacy

24n2   *No matter the circumstance:* Viktor E. Frankl, *Man's Search for Meaning: An Introduction to Logotherapy* (New York: Simon & Schuster, 1984), 75.

25   *Miroslav Volf talked about soldiers targeting and killing his brother:* Miroslav Volf, "Consider Forgiveness." Fetzer Institute: YouTube video, 7:26, September 22, 2009. https://www.youtube .com/watch?v=x8fbjzQcTws

27   *Most people do not listen with the intent to understand:* Stephen R. Covey, *The 7 Habits of Highly Effective People: Powerful Lessons in Personal Change* (New York: Simon & Schuster, 1989), 239.

Chapter Three

31   *Erwin McManus once tried to illustrate:* Erwin McManus, *Uprising* audio sermon series. Los Angeles: Mosaic.

37n1   *Where can you run to escape from yourself?:* Switchfoot. 2002. "Dare You To Move," track 1 on *Learning to Breathe*, San Diego: re:think Records.

37n2   *Man is a clever animal:* David Ives and David Valone, *Reverence for Life Revisited: Albert Schweitzer's Relevance Today* (Newcastle, UK: Cambridge Scholars Publishing, 2007), 12.

37n3   *Man is condemned to be free:* Jean-Paul Sartre, *Being and Nothingness: An Essay on Phenomenological Ontology* (New York: Kensington Publishing, 1956), 529.

39   *How do you know you're a leader? If someone is following you:* John Maxwell, *How Successful People Lead* (New York: Center Street Hachette, 1982), 20.

41n1   *This generation of children and teens:* Tim Elmore, *Generation Z Unfiltered: Facing Nine Hidden Challenges of the Most Anxious Population* (Atlanta: Poet Gardener Publishing, 2019), 28.

41n2   *People Are Taking Emotional Support Animals Everywhere:* Farah Stockman, "People Are Taking Emotional Support Animals Everywhere. States Are Cracking down." *The New York Times*, June 18, 2019.

Chapter Four

49 *Potiphar's wife was like Visa:* Elliott, Stuart. "Visa Trims Slogan to Expand Meaning." *The New York Times*, January 13, 2014.

56 **Dr. Manuel Rauchholz tells the story:** Dr. Manuel Rauchholz, story shared with permission.

Chapter Five

61n1 *Hope is being able to see:* Desmond Tutu, in "Questions for Archbishop Desmond Tutu: The Priest," *The New York Times Magazine*, March 4, 2010. https://www.nytimes.com/2010/03/07/magazine/07fob-q4-t.html

61n2 **The Washington Post reported on the story of a man who was told he had leukemia**: Sandra Boodman, "He Beat Leukemia but then Mysteriously Things Got Really Bad." Washington D.C., *The Washington Post*, June 6, 2016. https://www.washingtonpost.com/national/health-science/he-beat-leukemia-but-then-mysteriously-things-got-really-bad/2016/06/06/1178d9f0-0564-11e6-a12f-ea5aed7958dc_story.html

62 *Corrie ten Boom recalled a story and a prayer:* Corrie Ten Boom, John L. Sherrill, and Elizabeth Sherrill, *The Hiding Place* (Old Tappan, N.J.: Spire Books, 1971), 138.

64 *Bible commentator K. A. Mathews made a keen observation:* K. A. Mathews, "Genesis 11:27-50:26." *The New American Commentary*, vol. 1B (Nashville: Broadman & Holman, 2005), 745–752.

70 *At a certain point in the spiritual journey:* Richard J. Foster and James Bryan Smith, *Devotional Classics: Selected Readings for Individuals and Groups* (New York: HarperCollins, 1990), 33–39.

72 *One study showed that the wealthier people become:* Lindsay Dodgson, "Rich People Really Are Less Generous Than the Poor, Study Says." *Business Insider*, July 2, 2018. https://www.sciencealert.com/lower-status-people-more-likely-to-share-wealth-than-higher-status-people

Chapter Six

75 *I must first have the sense of God's possession of me:* Watchman Nee, *The Normal Christian Life* (Carol Stream, IL: Tyndale House, 1977), 42.

82 *Tony Campolo wrote a famous sermon and book:* Tony Campolo, *It's Friday, but Sunday's Coming!* (Nashville: Thomas Nelson Publishers, 1984)

Chapter Seven

87 *Country singer Tim McGraw says he lives by "one key value":* Samantha Kubota, "Tim McGraw lost 40 pounds after his daughter noticed he looked 'big,'" *NBC Today*, Oct. 29, 2019. https://www.today.com/health/tim-mcgraw-lost-40-pounds-after-his-daughter-noticed-he-t166029

88 *Dr. Erwin Lutzer tells of the moment:* Erwin Lutzer, *He Will Be the Preacher* (Chicago: Moody Publishers, 2015), 13–14.

90 *Albert-László Barabási has demonstrated that this number is likely less:* Albert-László Barabási, *Linked: How Everything Is Connected to Everything Else and What It Means for Business, Science, and Everyday Life* (New York: Perseus Books, 2002), 27–30.

103 *Out of the Grey once sang:* Out of the Grey. 1991. "He Is Not Silent," track 5 on *Out of the Grey*, Nashville, TN: Sparrow Records.

Chapter Eight

105 *Happiness is having a large, loving, caring, close-knit family:* George Burns, in *The Mammoth Book of Zingers, Quips, and One-Liners*, ed. Geoff Tibballs (New York: Carroll and Graf Publishers, 2004), 251.

111n1 *Robert Downey Jr. presented Shia LeBeouf:* Robert Downey Jr., "Robert Downey Jr. presents the Hollywood Breakthrough Screenwriter Award for Shia Labeouf," *Hollywood Film Awards*, Nov 3, 2019. https://www.youtube.com/watch?v=bEvNRIGcDMo

111n2 *It was coined and articulated by psychiatrist Dr. Stephen Karpman*: Stephen Karpman, "Fairy tales and script drama analysis," *Transactional Analysis Bulletin*, 1968, 26 (7): 39–43. https://en.wikipedia.org/wiki/Karpman_drama_triangle

111n3 *here's an excerpt from the* **Sydney Morning Herald***:* Sarah Berry, "The drama triangle: how to break the cycle of toxic relationships," *The Sydney Morning Herald*, Sydney, Australia: March 17, 2015. https://www.smh.com.au/lifestyle/the-drama-triangle-how-to-break-the-cycle-of-toxic-relationships-20150317-1m19gt.html

117 *Robin Williams was wildly successful but struggled:* Maria Puente, "What could have led Robin Williams to suicide?" *USA Today*, Nov. 11, 2014. https://www.usatoday.com/story/life/people/2014/11/11/what-could-have-led-robin-williams-to-suicide/18870615/

118 *With every loss, there are choices:* Henri Nouwen, "Passages to Life, Nov. 9," *You Are the Beloved: Daily Meditations for Spiritual Living* (New York: Convergent Books, 2017), 343.

Chapter Nine

121 *A family is a place where principles are hammered:* Charles R. Swindoll, *Standing Out: Being Real in an Unreal World* (Colorado Springs: Multnomah Press, 1979), 13.

123 *How often do people start down a path:* Angela Duckworth, *Grit: The Power of Passion and Perseverance* (New York: Scribner, 2016), 50.

129 *sometimes we "forgive in droplets":* Miroslav Volf, "Consider Forgiveness" Fetzer Institute, 2009: YouTube video, 7:26, September 22, 2009. https://www.youtube.com/watch?v=x8fbjzQcTws

Chapter Ten

137n1 *We name the colors of things we want to talk about:* Ted Gibson and Bevil R. Conway, "Languages don't all have the same number of terms for colors – scientists have a new theory why." *The Conversation*, September 18, 2017. https://theconversation.com/languages-dont-all-have-the-same-number-of-terms-for-colors-scientists-have-a-new-theory-why-84117

137n2   *different cultures have differing numbers of words for colors:* Alicia Brady, "7 Facts About Colors in Other Languages," *K-International*, November 27, 2016. https://k-international.com/blog/colors-in-other-languages/

139n1   *discover the boundaries of social interaction:* Henry Cloud and John Townsend, *Boundaries: When to Say Yes, How to Say No to Take Control of Your Life* (Grand Rapids, MI: Zondervan, 1992).

139n2   *Millennials Are the Therapy Generation:* Peggy Drexler, "Millennials Are the Therapy Generation," *The Wall Street Journal*, March 1, 2019. https://www.wsj.com/articles/millennials-are-the-therapy-generation-11551452286

139n3   *A prominent US pastor said:* Victoria Osteen, "Victoria Osteen, may God have mercy on your soul," *YouTube*, September 5, 2014. https://www.youtube.com/watch?v=fIVVJB9D5q8&feature=youtu.be

Chapter Eleven

150n1   *Otokitchi:* Bonny Tan, "Singapore's First Japanese Resident: Yamamoto Otokichi," *BiblioAsia Magazine*, vol. 12, issue 2, Jul-Sept. 2016. http://www.nlb.gov.sg/biblioasia/2016/07/07/singapores-first-japanese-resident-yamamoto-otokichi/

150n2   *Otokitchi:* Wikipedia, "Otokichi," last modified May 3, 2020. https://en.wikipedia.org/wiki/Otokichi

150n3   *helping him translate the Gospel of John:* Liana Lupus, (curator), "John in Japanese (Singapore, 1837)," *Rare Bible Collection @ MOBIA*, July 17, 2013. https://rarebiblesatmobia.wordpress.com/2013/07/17/john-in-japanese-singapore-1837/

157n1   *Victor Frankl, a concentration camp survivor, once wrote:* Viktor E. Frankl, *Man's Search for Meaning*, 1959 Boston: Beacon Press.

157n2   *People who suffer from maladaptive daydreaming:* Wikipedia, "Maladaptive daydreaming," last modified May 26, 2020. https://en.wikipedia.org/wiki/Maladaptive_daydreaming

172 *True humility is not thinking less of yourself:* Rick Warren, *The Purpose-Driven Life* (Grand Rapids, MI: Zondervan, 2002), 1.

173n1   *As long as you are proud you cannot know God:* C. S. Lewis, *Mere Christianity* (New York: HarperCollins, 1952), 124.

173n2   *I have been driven many times upon my knees:* Noah Brooks, "Personal Recollections of Abraham Lincoln," *Harpers New Monthly Magazine*, XXXI: 222, July, 1865.

Chapter Twelve

175 *Since we are all prone to live selfishly:* Helen Keller Quotes. BrainyQuote.com, BrainyMedia Inc, 2020. https://www.brainyquote.com/quotes/helen_keller_101340, accessed May 27, 2020.

176 *Hinds Feet on High Places:* Hannah Hurnard, *Hind's Feet on High Places* (London: Christian Literature Crusade, 1955).

180n1   *When William Borden was young:* Howard Taylor, *Borden of Yale*, Men of Faith Series (Bloomington, MN: Bethany House, 1988).

180n2   *Jim and Elizabeth Elliot left as missionaries to South America:* Elizabeth Elliot (ed.), *The Journals of Jim Elliot* (Grand Rapids, MI: Revell, 1978).

ABOUT PARACLETE PRESS

Who We Are

As the publishing arm of the Community of Jesus, Paraclete Press presents a full expression of Christian belief and practice—from Catholic to Evangelical, from Protestant to Orthodox, reflecting the ecumenical charism of the Community and its dedication to sacred music, the fine arts, and the written word. We publish books, recordings, sheet music, and video/DVDs that nourish the vibrant life of the church and its people.

What We Are Doing

BOOKS | PARACLETE PRESS BOOKS show the richness and depth of what it means to be Christian. While Benedictine spirituality is at the heart of who we are and all that we do, our books reflect the Christian experience across many cultures, time periods, and houses of worship.

We have many series, including *Paraclete Essentials*; *Paraclete Fiction*; *Paraclete Poetry*; *Paraclete Giants*; and for children and adults, *All God's Creatures*, books about animals and faith; and *San Damiano Books*, focusing on Franciscan spirituality. Others include *Voices from the Monastery* (men and women monastics writing about living a spiritual life today), *Active Prayer*, and new for young readers: *The Pope's Cat*. We also specialize in gift books for children on the occasions of Baptism and First Communion, as well as other important times in a child's life, and books that bring creativity and liveliness to any adult spiritual life.

The MOUNT TABOR BOOKS series focuses on the arts and literature as well as liturgical worship and spirituality; it was created in conjunction with the Mount Tabor Ecumenical Centre for Art and Spirituality in Barga, Italy.

MUSIC | PARACLETE PRESS DISTRIBUTES RECORDINGS of the internationally acclaimed choir *Gloriæ Dei Cantores*, the *Gloriæ Dei Cantores Schola*, and the other instrumental artists of the *Arts Empowering Life Foundation*.

PARACLETE PRESS IS THE EXCLUSIVE NORTH AMERICAN DISTRIBUTOR for the Gregorian chant recordings from St. Peter's Abbey in Solesmes, France. Paraclete also carries all of the Solesmes chant publications for Mass and the Divine Office, as well as their academic research publications.

In addition, PARACLETE PRESS SHEET MUSIC publishes the work of today's finest composers of sacred choral music, annually reviewing over 1,000 works and releasing between 40 and 60 works for both choir and organ.

VIDEO | Our video/DVDs offer spiritual help, healing, and biblical guidance for a broad range of life issues including grief and loss, marriage, forgiveness, facing death, understanding suicide, bullying, addictions, Alzheimer's, and Christian formation.

Learn more about us at our website:
www.paracletepress.com
or phone us toll-free at 1.800.451.5006

SCAN
TO
READ

YOU MAY ALSO BE INTERESTED IN THESE...

The Neglected C. S. Lewis
*Exploring the Riches of
His Most Overlooked Books*

Jerry Root and Mark Neal
Foreword by Dr. David Downing

ISBN 978-1-64060-294-6
Trade paperback | $24

The Gospel for the Person Who Has Everything

Will Willimon
Foreword by Lillian Daniel

ISBN 978-1-64060-540-4
Trade paperback | $16.99

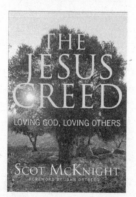

The Jesus Creed
Loving God, Loving Others

Scot McKnight
Foreword by John Ortberg

ISBN 978-1-61261-578-3
Trade paperback | $16.99